CREATIVE BIBLE LESSONS IN Psalms

Raw faith & rich praise
12 sessions from Israel's national songbook

CREATIVE BIBLE LESSONS IN Psalms

Raw faith & rich praise
12 sessions from Israel's national songbook

TIM BAKER

A DIVISION OF HARPERCOLLINSPUBLISHERS

Creative Bible Lessons in Psalms: Raw faith & rich praise — 12 sessions from Israel's national songbook

Youth Specialties Books, 300 S. Pierce St., El Cajon, CA 92020, are published by Zondervan Publishing House, 5300 Patterson Ave. S.E., Grand Rapids, MI 49530.

Library of Congress Cataloging-in-Publication Data

Baker, Tim, 1965-
Creative Bible lessons in Psalms : raw faith & rich praise : 12 sessions from Israel's national songbook / Tim Baker.
p. cm.
ISBN 0-310-23178-7
1. Bible. O.T. Psalms — Commentaries. 2. Bible. O.T. Psalms — Study and teaching. 3. Youth — Religious life. I. Title.
BS1430.3 .B35 2000
223'.2'00712 — dc
00-036792

Edited by Crystal Kirgiss and Lory Floyd
Cover and interior design by Jack Rogers Design

Printed in the United States of America

02 03 04 05 06 / VG / 10 9 8 7 6 5 4 3

CONTENTS

ACKNOWLEDGMENTS

Special thanks to—

The Youth Specialties product development team—Tim, Vicki, Mary, Karla, Mark. You're the absolute best to work with. Thanks for your patience and support. You're truly wonderful people. (Psalm 146)

The youth and college students at Hope Fellowship. You're always so willing to try new and weird ideas. Thank you for your encouragement, enthusiasm, and trust. (Psalm 91)

Nicole and Jessica. I hope someday you realize the mystical, wonderful, honest, raw, and saving message that's in the Psalms. You're everything a dad could want in his kids. (Psalms 121 and 127)

Jacqui. This book belongs to you. (Psalm 126:1-3)

INTRO

What this book is all about, and how to use it

Imagine that an accomplished artist, a painter, has requested your presence for an evening meal. The only thing is, you don't know beans about art—and besides, your week is packed with a full schedule of lock-ins, small-group meetings, staff retreats. The artist's request frustrates as much as flatters you, but at the urging of one of your former youth group students who's an art major, you accept—with the request to get her an autograph.

You show up early and discover that this famous artist has reserved an entire banquet hall just for the two of you. He's been there for hours. On one side of the hall are tables filled with delicate hors d'oeuvres, succulent entrees, sculpted desserts. On the other side of the hall hang paintings that look hauntingly familiar...until you realize that they're pictures of your life. There's your childhood...your spouse...even a few portraits of kids in your youth group.

There's also a large, empty canvas on an easel. "Fill your plate, then sit here," the artist says, gesturing to a chair. You obey. "We're not here to talk," he says. "But go ahead and eat."

For what seems like an hour, the painter sits and stares at you. Then he rises, approaches the easel, dips his hands into his paints, and begins daubing paint onto the canvas. But what starts as smeary colors begins to take forms and shapes that you recognize. Is that...it *is* Jason, the sophomore in your group who got caught last year smoking pot. You haven't seen him since—well, for a long time. In fact, the artist's way of capturing Jason's emotions moves you, and you feel your eyes get wet. For Jason. Then you recognize Hannah...a rough start, but what a change you saw in her—a street kid who you helped get into a halfway house and, finally, a home of her own.

In this way the artist paints face after face, person after person. And then comes an image your recognize to be your own. He captures even the frustration you've held for so long. There's a hint of joy in your painted expression, but only a hint. It's been a while since you've felt much outright joy. But he captures you accurately.

"How did you know?" you ask him. Then you see the scars on his wrists.

The writers of the Psalms had experiences something like this. All of them sat down to canvases, and then watched God paint. What emerged on the canvases made them recall God's acts. In glorious moments, when they actually saw God creating, they wrote it down. When they didn't see God painting, they panicked. The writers of 150 songs collected in the Hebrew Bible, or Old Testament, and called "the Psalms" used words, of course, not paint. But their portrayals are no less graphic or familiar. They're vibrant pictures of struggling believers—paintings of people stretching to reach the Holy, verbal paint smears of people who felt alone, abused, and abandoned. And splashes of joy, thanksgiving, and praise.

They're pictures of us.

The aim of *Creative Bible Lessons in Psalms* is to help your students understand the meaning and message that each psalm contains.

And because you've got very real kids in very real situations—nothing theoretical or particularly typical about your youth group—a lot of options fill each lesson, options that let you combine, connect, or conclude however you want. Pick and choose the elements you want in a lesson.

• First comes an introduction to the *kind* of psalm that lesson is about—blessing psalms, complaint psalms, royal psalms, whatever:

Stepping Back

This section is generally for you: some big-picture background...historical, cultural, or theological insight...and maybe, if your students are budding Bible scholars, some details to work into your lesson.

Opener. Actually, *two* openers are usually offered—one is generally more involved (meaning you'll probably need to gather more supplies, copy some handouts, do three back flips, or arrange for some special something-or-other before the lesson), the other is simpler to prep for.

Whichever option you choose, this first activity is key to getting students involved in the lesson. It's a hook to get students into the psalm and into your subject.

In the Book. Here's the Bible study part of the lesson.

What it all means. Two or three options wait for you here: the typical entrees are an activity, a small-group discussion, and/or a straightforward talk you can give. Each option takes a little different tack on the psalm under study. (The talks can also be used as stand-alone devotionals.)

Closing. Like any effective closing, this section asks, *What would this truth look like if I tried to make it work in my life?* You'll find creative discussion starters, group closing activities, personal commitment times—all geared to help your kids fit the truth of the psalm to their lives or discuss how their lives need to change in order to fit the truth.

And finally, a few details before you take the plunge:

•Yes, the lessons spell out just about everything for you, including what to say and when to say it. But don't think that you can walk in cold to a classroom and teach an effective lesson without preparing. Of course, the more experienced a teacher or youth worker you are, the less you'll need to prep. But do whatever prep you need. Read the listed psalms. Read through the lesson. Choose ahead of time which options you'll use. Ask yourself, *What will make this lesson connect with my students?*

• Don't feel bound to this book, or any instructions in it. Tweak the ideas here to make them your own. Lose the options that you know won't work with your kids. Change the order, use your own words—in short, make the lesson your own.

• If you're going to use the leader-talk option, don't read it (although it's there for you in each lesson, word for word). Read through the talk *before* your meeting, capture the gist of the talk, and deliver it in your own words. Or write out the ideas on an index card or two. Or memorize the main points that you can talk from.

• Permit the unseen to happen. After all, the Psalms are all about a more-often-than-not invisible God moving, shaking, working, saving, rescuing, and loving people who ached just like we do for his presence. This same God longs to invade your students. So let it happen. ◆

What the Psalms are, where they came from, and how to read them for all they're worth

The Book of Psalms

So you want to study the Psalms, eh? Or maybe you don't really want to, but you're being pressured to include some Old Testament stuff in your program and Psalms seems like the easiest. After all, who wants to study the prophets or the judges or the chronicles and genealogies of stuffy kings?

Nope, it'll be the Psalms for you, all those nice little poems about praising God in the sanctuary, lying down by still waters, delighting in the Lord.

And being oppressed, seeking vengeance on enemies, feeling totally abandoned by everyone and everything.

Hmm...well, maybe the Psalms isn't merely a book of nice little poems at all. Maybe it's something much deeper, much richer, much more important. Maybe it's exactly what your kids need to be studying. In that case, kudos to you for such a fine and well-thought-out choice of topics.

As you begin this study, keep several things in mind—beside the fact that Psalms is a whole lot more than a collection of nice little poems.

First, Psalms is primarily a book of songs and prayers. True, each one deals with some pretty heavy and real issues that may very well relate to your kids, such as loneliness, fear, and anger. But ultimately Psalms does not teach its readers *about* these issues. It's no theological treatise, but rather a book that teaches us how to *pray* and *praise* when we find ourselves in the same situations and facing the same issues as the psalmists.

Second, we don't know a lot about the Psalms beyond this—

- It was written by many different people, including David, some of whom we know nothing about.
- It was written over a broad time period extending from before to after the Jewish exile, and it was probably compiled in its present form sometime during the third century B.C.
- It was used regularly in worship for both praying and singing, and many of the words such as *Selah* probably had to do with performance or liturgical directions.

Stepping Back

We all need a good dose of authentic faith. The Psalms reassure us that authentic faith is possible in the midst of everything life throws our way.

Chances are your students are pretty New Testament oriented. The New Testament is where it's at, right? Grace, salvation, parables...all the good stuff, all the relevant stuff is there.

But all that good stuff, all that relevant stuff, is part of a whole. And included in that whole is the book of Psalms. At one time, Psalms was the where-it's-at part of God's Word. As the national prayer book and songbook of the Old Testament-era temple, the Jews were as familiar with the Psalms as we are with the New Testament. New Testament writers quoted the Psalms frequently. Jesus himself quoted the Psalms regularly. Obviously, the Psalms have something important to say.

The problem is this—the Psalms don't always say things in a straightfor-

continued next page

Third, if there is one underlying theme to the entire book of Psalms, it is this—there is one God who is in charge of all creation, all history, all everything. As one commentator put it, "At the core of the theology of the Psalter is the conviction that the gravitational center of life...is God" (*NIV Study Bible*).

> Before going any further it might be helpful for you to read more about the book of Psalms. Check out the introduction in any study Bible. Or get your hands on a Bible handbook. If you want something more meaty, check out C. S. Lewis's *Reflections on the Psalms,* Eugene Peterson's *Answering God,* or A. F. Kirkpatrick's *The Book of Psalms.*

During these lessons, your students will read and study the innermost thoughts of historical people who experienced and felt many of the same things they do today—feeling bad about making some really big mistakes, feeling angry, feeling left out of the crowd, feeling abandoned, feeling resentful, feeling afraid, feeling unsure...you name it and the psalmists felt it. Just like your kids. Just like you.

So get ready to deal with real people, real life, and real faith. Because this ain't just another book of nice little poems—not by a long shot.

Stepping Back *(cont.)*

ward, clear-cut manner that's immediately grasped. The writers were not merely relating events or recording conversations but, rather, were writing from their hearts—opening themselves up to God completely in order to listen to him and then respond accordingly.

It makes sense that reading the Psalms requires the same creativity, open-mindedness, and open-heartedness expressed by the psalmists themselves. This lesson will help your students with that.

▶▶▶Opener (artsy option)▶▶▶▶▶▶▶▶▶▶▶▶▶▶▶▶▶▶▶▶

"Me," by me

You'll need...
- blank paper
- markers
- tape or tacks for posting artwork

When everyone has arrived have students find a place in the room where they can have some privacy. Give each student two sheets of paper and some markers. Begin with something like this—

> **Today I'd like you to think of yourselves as artists. On one of the sheets of paper I gave you, I'd like you to draw a picture of your life. You can use pictures, words, symbols...anything that comes to mind. Don't worry—you won't be graded on your artistic ability. Leave the other sheet blank.**

Give students time to draw their pictures. Then have them hang their drawings and their blank sheets of paper side-by-side on the walls of the meeting room. Ask them to walk around the room and look at the other pictures. On the blank sheets of paper, ask them to write down titles for the picture beside it. When students are finished, send them back to find their own pictures to read the titles that others gave them. Have them share the results with the rest of the class. Then ask these questions.

- **What did you notice about other people's drawings?**
- **What title did you like the best? Why?**
- **Is it easy for you to share honestly about your life? Why?**

> Students might have difficulty with this opener because it's ambiguous. That's okay. It's intended to be somewhat vague so students can share whatever comes to mind. If a student appears to be really struggling, offer some suggestions along the lines of hobbies, important dates, important places, etc.

▸▸▸ Opener (writing option) ▸▸▸▸▸▸▸▸▸▸▸▸▸▸▸▸▸▸▸▸

The real me

You'll need...
- copies of **The Real Me** (page 20)
- pencils

When students have settled down, say something like this—

> **Today we're going to begin a journey studying some pretty intense folks who wrote honestly about themselves and their lives. But before we start, I'd like you to think about your own lives for a moment.**

Distribute copies of **The Real Me** (page 20) and ask your students to write in their answers. When they're finished ask them to put their answers into poetry—not necessarily the rhyming kind, but something that reads more fluidly than straight answers. Explain by saying something like this—

> **Lots of people keep a journal as a way to talk about themselves and express their feelings. I'd like you to take your answers from the worksheet and put them into a journaling-poetry format. For example, you might write something like—**
>
> ***Everyday it's the same***
> ***Never enough time to be myself***
> ***Always too busy trying to be someone else***
> ***I feel lonely, happy, sad all at the same time***
> ***Never sure where I want to go...***
>
> **Whatever you write is fine. I just want you to be as honest as you can.**

When students have finished writing, have them form groups of four to share their responses to the questions. If they feel comfortable they can also share the poems-psalms they wrote. After they've shared, ask the following questions.

- **Did your poem represent your life? How?**
- **Is it easy for you to express the details of your life with other people? Explain.**
- **When have you felt angry at God or happy about your relationship with him, but you weren't sure how to express yourself?**

Regardless of the opener you use, transition into the next section with something like this—

> **Today we're going to begin looking at a book of the Bible that a lot of people tend to ignore or never really study too closely, the book of Psalms. As we walk through this book, you'll learn a lot about how people communicated with God a long time ago, what they believed about him, and how they lived out their beliefs.**

In the Book

Getting technical

You'll need...
- copies of **A Psalmatic Survey** (page 18)
- pencils
- Bibles

While students form groups of four, distribute pencils and copies of the **A Psalmatic Survey** (page 18). Make sure each group also has a Bible. Instruct groups to read each psalm listed on the handout and then write what they think it's about in the appropriate box. When they're finished have each group join another to compare their responses. Finally, invite students to gather in the center of the meeting room and ask volunteers to share their responses with the entire group.

If you have a small group, consider having students pair up.

Continue the lesson with something like this—

Let's experiment. I'm going to read something to you and I'd like you to recall what you just learned from the Psalms. Think about what the Psalms might say about these situations.

Begin reading these situations and give students time to respond.

- **Rafael has been having trouble getting along with his parents. It's not that they have serious fights all the time—it's just that they disagree about everything. Lately, he's been having trouble sleeping.**
- **Leslie and Terry have been dating for years. Last night Terry pressured Leslie to go too far. At first Leslie said no, but after awhile she finally gave in. Now she feels terrible.**

- **Taylor smoked pot for the first time last night. His first few hits made him feel sick. After a while, though, he started to feel really strange. He tried driving home, but he hit a parked car. Now he's in jail.**
- **Ireland has been trying to get closer to God lately. She's even been having private worship times. But no matter how hard she tries, she still feels disconnected from God.**

After reading these situations and giving students time to apply the Psalms to the situations, ask—

Do the psalms you've read today apply to your life? How?

▸▸▸What it all means (discussion option)▸▸▸▸▸▸▸▸▸▸▸

You'll need...
- copies of **What's Up With This Psalm** (page 19) cut into strips
- pencils

What's up with this Psalm?

Have students pair up and then have the pairs link up with another pair to create a group of four. Begin this section with something like this—

> **I'd like you to discuss what impact the Psalms you talked about might have on your life.**

Give a question strip from **What's Up with This Psalm** (page 19) to each pair of students to discuss. After a few minutes ask all pairs to link up with another pair to form a new group of four. Ask the new quads to discuss the responses their group gave during the small group time.

Wrap up the discussion by saying—

> **Remember, the psalms were written by real people. God was working in their lives long ago, and he works in our lives today.**

▸▸▸What it all means (leader-talk option)▸▸▸▸▸▸▸▸▸▸▸

You'll need...
- 3 Bibles opened to Psalm 78, Psalm 13, and Psalm 139

Real history, real emotions, real relationships

Explain to students that the only way to understand the Psalms is to realize that they deal with real people, real events, and real emotions.

- **The Psalms reveal the history of real people.**

  Ask a student to read Psalm 78:13-22 from one of the Bibles.

  Explain that a key ingredient in the Psalms is the historical information found there. The Psalms not only record what people did—they also record God's interaction with them. Say something like—

  > **When people talked to God in the Psalms, they talked about real things that had happened. It was important to them to look back on their history as a way of remembering how God had worked in their lives and as a reminder that he would continue to work in their future.**

- **The Psalms reveal the emotions of real people.**

  Ask a student to read Psalm 13:1-6 from one of the Bibles.

  Explain to your students that not only did the Psalms deal with real events but they also dealt with real emotions. Say something like—

  > **When people talked to God in the Psalms, they were completely honest with him. They didn't hide their emotions from him. If they were angry, they said so. If they were mad, they said so. The**

emotions may not have always been positive or justified, but they knew that God would listen to them anyway. God promises to listen to us whenever we talk to him, not just when we're happy and feeling close to him, but also when we're struggling or upset.

- **The Psalms reveal real relationships with a real God.**
  Ask a student to read Psalm 139:1-12 from one of the Bibles.
  Explain to your students that the writers of the psalms assumed that there was someone listening on the other end. Why? Because they had a relationship with that someone, God, and they knew him well enough to trust that he was listening. Say something like—

The people who wrote the psalms weren't writing just for the sake of writing. They were communicating with a God they knew and trusted and had a relationship with. Which is what God wants with you—a real relationship that involves communication, getting to know one another, and genuine intimacy.

▶▶▶Closing ▶▶▶▶▶▶▶▶▶▶▶▶▶▶▶▶▶▶▶▶▶▶▶▶▶▶▶

Prayer for help and guidance

Conclude with something like this—

We've seen a lot in the Psalms today about real people who had a relationship with God. More than anything else the Psalms are prayers and songs that can teach us how to talk to and listen to God in any circumstance. Let's end tonight by doing just that—praying.

Lead your students in the following litany. Teach them the student response (it's simple enough that they should have it down after a couple practice recitations), and during the prayer cue them when they should respond. (This litany is based on Psalm 25: 4-5.)

leader
God, you are the One who created us, as you created David and the other writers who wrote these psalms to you in worship and praise.

students
Show us your ways, O Lord, and teach us your paths.

leader
We thank you for hearing not just our thanks and requests, but also our complaints and frustrations.

students
Show us your ways, O Lord, and teach us your paths.

leader

We tell you now, God, that we want to understand more of this book of Psalms, so that we can love you more and love each other better.

students

Show us your ways, O Lord, and teach us your paths.

leader

Guide us in your truth and teach us, for you are God our Savior, and our hope is in you all day long.

students

Show us your ways, O Lord, and teach us your paths.

all

Amen.

A Psalmatic Survey (or, the Great Psalm-a-Rama)

Passage	What it means
Psalm 1:1–6	
Psalm 11:1–7	
Psalm 13:1–6	
Psalm 83:1–18	
Psalm 116:1–7	
Psalm 128:1–6	
Psalm 136:1–26	

WHAT'S UP WITH THIS PSALM?

HOW DOES THE MATERIAL IN THESE PSALMS APPLY TO YOUR LIFE?

IF YOU LIVED THE WAY THESE PSALMS DESCRIBE, WHAT MIGHT CHANGE IN YOUR LIFE?

HOW WERE THE PSALMISTS' LIVES DIFFERENT FROM YOURS?

WHAT PSALM STANDS OUT TO YOU THE MOST? WHY?

WHICH PSALM SEEMS THE MOST UNBELIEVABLE?

WHAT DID YOU LEARN FROM DISCUSSING THESE PSALMS?

The Real Me

Three emotions I feel almost all of the time:

A time when I felt abandoned:

A time when I knew God was working in my life:

A time I sinned and felt really guilty:

A time I hated someone:

A time I felt extremely happy:

A time I felt angry at God:

Seeing God at work in your personal history **Psalm 105**

Torah Psalms

Unlike the many psalms that read like private, even intimate journal entries, Torah psalms sound more like decrees, edicts, and commands. But hidden within these decrees are words of instruction. Some impart wisdom, others share testimonies. Torah psalms often take a look at what went on in history and what's going on presently, then compare and contrast the two for the benefit of the listener or reader.

Torah comes from a word meaning *to shoot* or *to teach*. "When one man teaches another, he shoots ideas from his own into the other's mind," explains George A.F. Knight in *A Christian Theology of the Old Testament*. In fact, Torah Psalms sometimes sound like a shower of arrows being shot in the direction of the listener or reader: *Remember when God did this...don't forget when God did this...remember when God said this...don't forget when God said that...remember when you did this...don't forget when you did that.* You get the idea.

Many psalms are motivated and borne out of the writer's emotions. And usually, when you reflect on those emotions, you gain wisdom and knowledge. (More about this in later lessons.) The Torah Psalms, however, take exactly the opposite approach: the emotional response they deliver spring from actual events—historical, present-day, or otherwise. Or look at it another way: the first type of psalm moves from the emotional to the concrete; the second type, from the concrete to the emotional. (It's healthy to remember that our own faith also needs to move in both of these directions.) Some people think the Psalms deal only with sorrow, pain, suffering, happiness, and such feelings. They're wrong—Torah Psalms, among others, deal with hard, historical facts.)

More Torah Psalms–1, 32, 47, 127

The psalm in this study (105) reflects on the history of the Israelites in order to communicate the very concrete truth that *God is faithful to his promises.* Then the psalmist segues from the concrete truth to the deeply felt emotion *I love God and I want to praise him.*

Psalm 105 doesn't mind repeating the obvious. Everyone who listened to this psalm in the temple was probably very familiar with its content. *(Oh boy, the Egypt story again...isn't there something* new *we can*

Stepping Back

Everyone loves a good story. This psalm reminds us that God acts in our lives and that he'll keep working in and through our personal history.

History isn't a lot of fun for many people, especially those who are being forced to study it—like your students, for instance. Not only do many students hate history, but they don't *know* history, either. Ask them to date the major wars of the 20th century and be prepared for a blank stare. True, there are a few history buffs out there, but they're greatly outnumbered by the sports and music buffs.

So then why should you spend an entire lesson about the history of Israel? Good question. Here's a good answer: because it's in Scripture—and if it's in Scripture, it must be in there for a reason.

Besides, believe it or not, this psalm has a lot to offer you and your students.

For starters, your stu-

continued next page

Stepping Back *(cont.)*

dents each have a personal history. For the past 14 to 18 years, they've each walked the earth. They've had relationships. They've experienced upheaval. They've moved from place to place. They've gone through pain and hardship. They've had good times and bad times. They started as babies and now they're young adults. A lot has happened in between. This psalm will show your students that a person's history has something to offer beyond mere memories. *History gives us a glimpse of God working in our lives.*

Second, your students each have a collective history as children of God. As part of Christ's church, they need to know and be familiar with the history of salvation. That history closely parallels and is borne out of the history recounted in this psalm. In this single lesson you obviously aren't going to cover the entire Exodus, but you may whet your students' appetites to learn more about it on their own. Finally, the same God who worked in the lives of the Israelites centuries ago now works in the lives of your students. By studying God's actions and by observing how the psalmist responded to those actions, your students will learn more about how God works in their own lives today and how they can respond to him.

sing about this week?) But the psalmist knew better. He knew that it's okay to recall—privately and publicly—the carefully pondered acts of God in our lives. The good things God has done for us shouldn't be said once and then left behind. They're to be repeated over and over again—creatively, mind you, not *ad nauseam*—so that no one forgets. And in their repetition, things are learned.

Need a refresher course on Israel's history before teaching this lesson? Spend some time in the book of Exodus this week, especially chapters 1-17.

Human beings are complex creatures made up of, among other things, both feelings and thoughts. Scripture encourages us to worship God in spirit *and* truth. The Torah Psalms show us how to do that.

▸▸▸Opener (investigation option) ▸▸▸▸▸▸▸▸▸▸▸▸▸▸▸▸▸▸

Herb's history

You'll need...
- copies of **Herb's History** (page 27)

As students arrive, hand each of them a copy of **Herb's History** (page 27). When everyone is settled in, say something like this—

> **For just a moment, I want you to pretend that Herb, a very important member of our community, is missing. It's your job to recreate the last few hours before he disappeared by using a few receipts that were found in his car.**

Move your students into groups of three or four. Give the kids enough time to create their ideas of where they think Herb might be and what might have happened to him. When they're ready have groups present their ideas to the rest of the class. Ask them to explain how they arrived at their conclusions.

After each group has presented, ask them—

- **How easy was it to retrace Herb's history with only a few clues?**
- **How much could you learn about Herb personally from these few receipts?**
- **Is history important? Why?**
- **What can history teach us?**

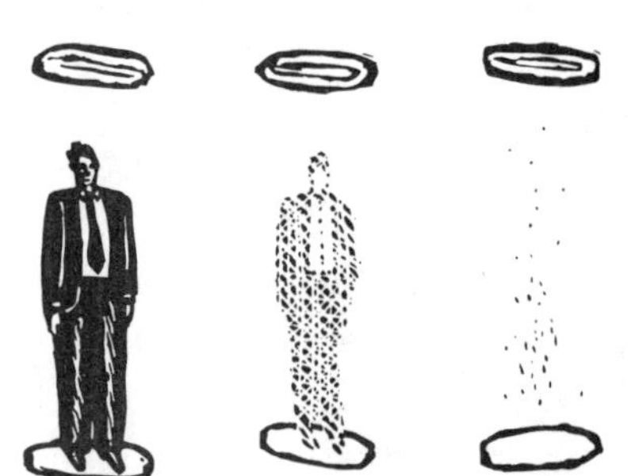

Obviously, your students can't retrace Herb's history with only a few receipts. But they can learn a few things about him as a person. Similarly, they won't be able to retrace the entire history of the Israelites simply by reading Psalm 105. But they will be able to learn some things about them and about God.

▸▸▸Opener (writing option)▸▸▸▸▸▸▸▸▸▸▸▸▸▸▸▸▸▸▸▸▸▸

You'll need...
- paper
- pencil

Where I've been

Begin this opener by saying something like this—

> **On your paper, make three lists. First, list six things you did yesterday, then list six things you did last month, and then list six things you did last year.**

After a few minutes, have students move into groups of four and read their lists to each other. Then ask them to discuss these questions as a group—

- **How did you choose which six things to include in each list?**
- **If someone only knew about six things in your past, would they have an accurate picture of you? Explain.**
- **What can history teach us?**

Close either of these openers with words like this—

> **History's an important thing. We've all been somewhere different. And each of us has a history with God. Today we're going to take a wild ride through the history of the Israelites. We're not going to learn everything about them, but we will learn about some significant events they were part of, we'll learn why they were thankful, and we'll learn how they expressed that thanks to God.**

▸▸▸In the Book▸▸▸▸▸▸▸▸▸▸▸▸▸▸▸▸▸▸▸▸▸▸▸▸▸

You'll need...
- a large sheet of butcher paper for each group
- markers
- Bibles

History lists

Introduce this section like this—

> **Before you dive into this psalm, I'd like you to remember one thing. The people who originally sang or recited this psalm were very familiar with the story it refers to. They could fill in all the blanks and details because they'd heard it many times. That may not be the case for all of us. Even if this story isn't familiar to you, there are things we can all learn from this psalm.**

Have students get in new groups of four to read Psalm 105. Give each group a large sheet of butcher paper and markers. After groups have finished reading it, have them make a list of all the historical events recorded. For example, in verse 9, God made a covenant with Abraham. In verse 16, famine took over the land. In verse 17, Joseph was sold into slavery. You may need to get them started with a few examples like these.

When they're finished have the groups look over their lists and discuss the following questions—

- **How do you think the psalmist decided what events to include?**
- **What can you tell about the relationship between the Israelites and God from this psalm?**
- **Why do you think this series of events was so important to the Israelites?**
- **What was the psalmist's response to this story? Look at verses 1-5 and 45.**

You'll need...
- copies of **My Life History** (page 28)
- pencils

▶▶▶What it all means (nostalgia option)▶▶▶▶▶▶▶▶▶▶▶

The history of my life

To open kids' eyes to God's presence in their lives, open the section like this—

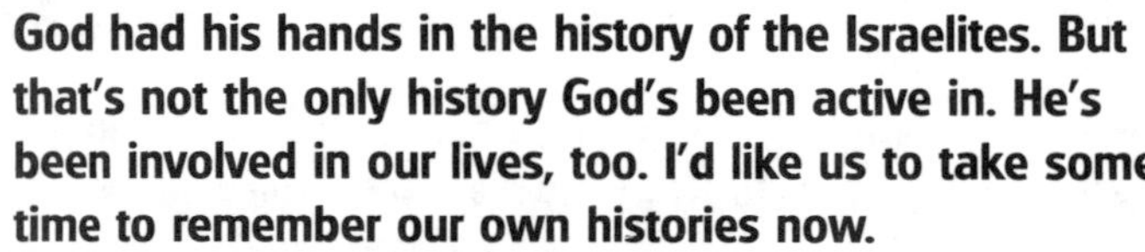

God had his hands in the history of the Israelites. But that's not the only history God's been active in. He's been involved in our lives, too. I'd like us to take some time to remember our own histories now.

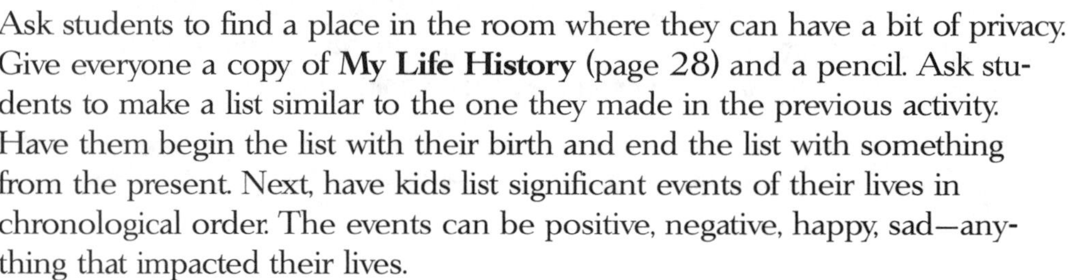

Ask students to find a place in the room where they can have a bit of privacy. Give everyone a copy of **My Life History** (page 28) and a pencil. Ask students to make a list similar to the one they made in the previous activity. Have them begin the list with their birth and end the list with something from the present. Next, have kids list significant events of their lives in chronological order. The events can be positive, negative, happy, sad—anything that impacted their lives.

After a few minutes ask students to go back through their lists and think about these things—

- **Where can I see God at work in my history, even if I didn't realize it at the time?**
- **What things am I thankful for in my history?**
- **What can I learn from looking back at things in my past?**

When students are finished, have them pair up to share what they wrote and what they've thought about.

You'll need...
- index cards

▶▶▶What it all means (leader-talk option)▶▶▶▶▶▶▶▶▶▶▶

Israel's history, my history

Prepare ahead of time by writing out a real-life situation that a few students will act out. Choose from the following, or create you own—

- Your mom comes home and asks you how your job interview went. You feel like she's always checking up on you and doesn't trust you. Pretty soon you're arguing about responsibilities, trust, curfew...

- Your younger brother borrowed one of your CDs yesterday without asking and accidentally lost it at school today. You feel like he's always taking your stuff without being careful. You confront him about it.

- Your friend meets you at your locker, visibly upset. She accuses you of gossiping about her, which in fact you did. You talk about what happened.

Ask for two volunteers to act out an impromptu skit for the group. Give them the skit card you wrote out and tell them that they've got 30 seconds to create a short skit based on the situation that you've given them. Students can go to the hallway or the room next door to practice.

While you wait for them to get ready, start your talk with something like this—

Sometimes the easiest way to see God at work in our lives is by looking backward at our past. We're able to see things in hindsight that we can't always see when we're in the middle of something. Why? Because later on our emotions aren't all tangled up. Or because we've matured. Or because we've learned more about God. Let's take a look at something that could easily happen to any one of us.

Invite your performers forward to act out their impromptu skit. After they've performed it once, start the applause and encourage your teens to join in. Then ask your performers to act it out again, but tell them when they hear *freeze* they're to freeze no matter what they're doing. Give them the signal to begin the skit again. Yell *freeze* after a few seconds. Then say something like this—

God observes our history.

At the time it may not seem like God is present when something difficult happens in our lives. Or if things are going good, we may forget that God is around because we don't feel like we really need him.

Have students look at the frozen actors and ask how they might be feeling and why it might be easy to forget that God is there. Then ask if they think the actors might feel differently about the situation at a later date and why.

Give your actors the signal to begin the skit where they left off. Let them act for another few seconds, then yell *freeze* again. Continue with something like—

God puts himself in our history.

As he did with the Israelites, God watches us, too. No matter

what we're doing, God is there. He's involved. He's interested in what's going on in our lives, even if it doesn't seem very exciting or important.

Have students look at the frozen actors again and ask them where they think God is in the skit or how he might be working in the events. Is he watching from afar? Is he right in the middle of it encouraging them to act a certain way?

Give your actors the signal to begin the skit once more where they left off. As they finish the skit, yell *freeze* one more time. Continue with something like this.

God longs for us to surrender our future.

God is actively involved in our lives—past, present, *and* future. One of the reasons it's important to look back at our past is so we can learn more about God and ourselves, and then use what we learn to help us in the future. What God wants more than anything is for us to trust him enough to surrender our futures to him, believing that he'll be right there with us in everything that happens.

Ask a student to read Jeremiah 29:11. Discuss how God knows us—our plans and what he's called us to. Remind students that our histories *and* our futures are extremely important to God.

You'll need...
- copies of **Past, Present, & Future** (page 29)
- pencils
- a small cardboard box

Closing

Past, present, & future

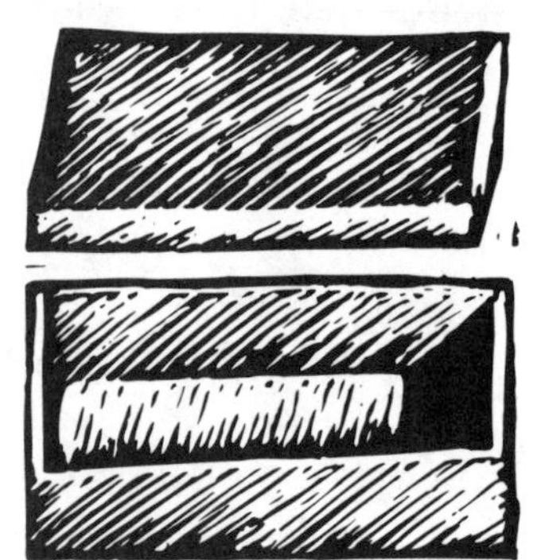

Give each student a copy of **Past, Present, & Future** and a pencil. Ask them to take a few minutes to think about the past five years of their lives, the present, and the next five years in their futures. Then have them fill in their sheets.

After they've had some time to work on this, say something like—

God has directed the history of your lives up to this point. He's been there for all of your good moments, as well as your bad. And he's going to be there for your futures.

Some students aren't comfortable praying aloud. Before you begin praying give them the option to pray silently before placing their sheets in the box.

Place the cardboard box on the floor and ask your group to gather around it. Spend a few moments with students sharing one-sentence prayers thanking God for his work in the past and asking him to guide their futures. After each prayer have them place their sheets in the box as a symbol of surrendering the past, present, and future to God. If you have students who might want to keep their **Past, Present, & Future** sheets, be sure to make that option available.

HERB'S HISTORY

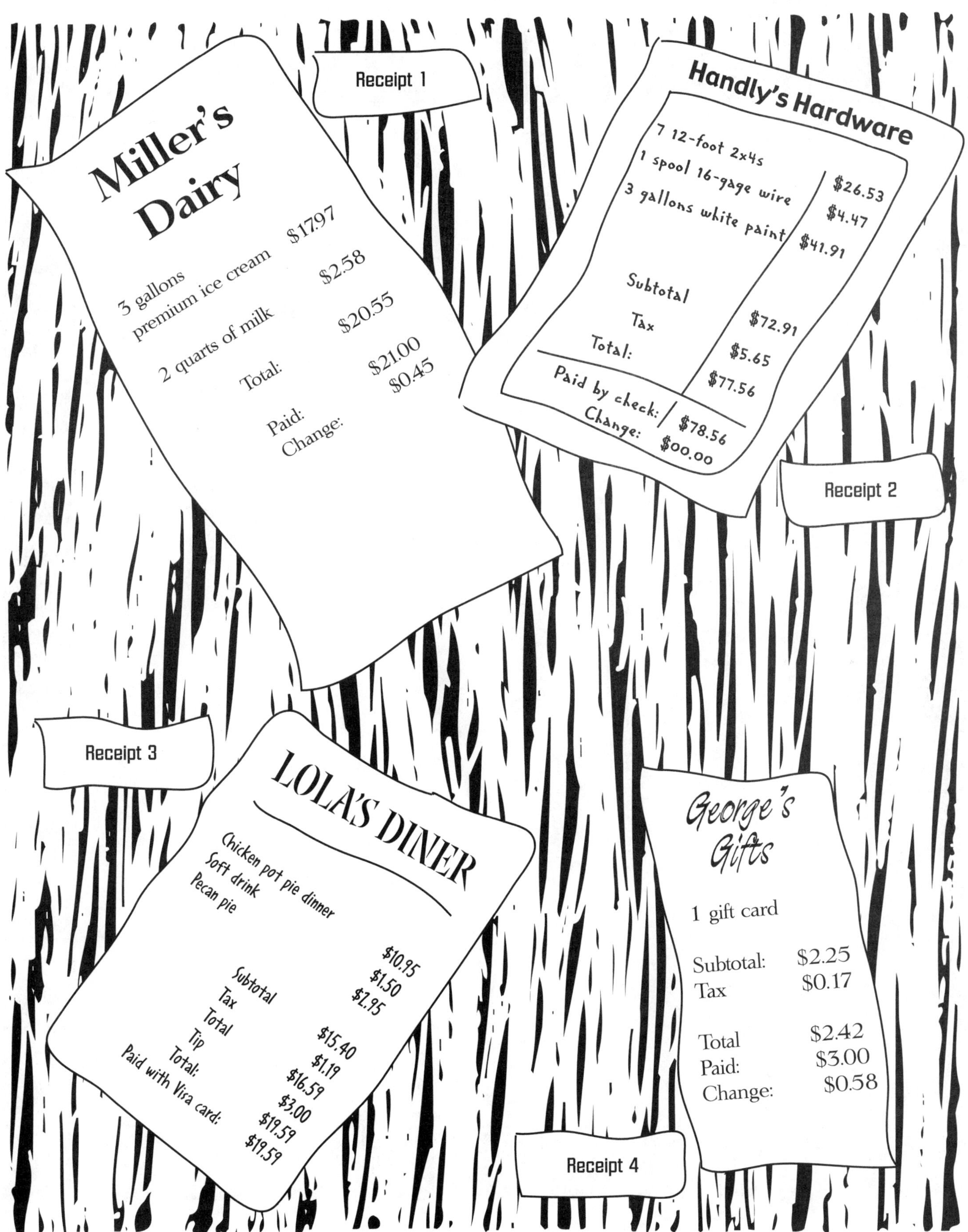

My Life History

Past, Present, & Future

Past

List ways you think God has worked in your life during the past five years.

Write a few sentences thanking God for what he's done in the past.

Present

List ways you think God is working in your life right now.

Write a few sentences thanking God for what he's doing in your life right now. If you need his help or guidance, include that also.

Future

List things that you hope to accomplish or experience in the next five years.

Write a few sentences about how you hope God will be involved in your future, based on what you've seen in the past and what you know about him.

A daily dose of blessings **Psalms 1 and 65**

Blessing Psalms

Ahh...the blessing psalms. They are a clear reminder of the incredible blessings God bestows on the world—sunshine, rain, crops, mountains, streams, grasslands. The list is infinite.

God's blessings are available and visible to everyone—the righteous and the unrighteous alike. The sun shines on the entire world. The streams deliver water to both sacred and pagan lands. The crops grow in fields tilled by both God's people and God's enemies.

God's blessings are not something we earn. God *bestows* his blessings—he does not pay them out. So what's the difference if a person is a God-follower or not when it comes to being blessed?

Simply this—though his blessings are not *earned* by any one person more than another, they are certainly *enjoyed* by the righteous more than the unrighteous. Why? Because the righteous are in a position to recognize God's blessings for what they really are—incredible gifts of love from the creator of the universe.

Interested in being blessed by more of these psalms? Look up Psalms 20, 67, and 128.

In addition to the psalms that list God's many blessings, there are numerous psalms that describe those who are blessed. In every case, the blessed ones are in a daily, intimate, and obedient relationship with God.

The unrighteous person gazes on creation and says, "Wow. Awesome. Beautiful stuff."

The righteous person gazes on creation and says, "Wow. Awesome. Beautiful stuff. God made all of this for me to enjoy? I can't believe it. I don't deserve it. I am humbled beyond words."

It's a small and subtle difference, yes, but one that changes a person's life drastically.

Stepping Back

We enjoy the blessings of God when we are living as blessed people. We live as blessed people when we have growing, active relationships with God. We have growing, active relationships with God when we spend time with him each day.

No doubt you've talked with your students about spending time with God each day. In fact, you've probably talked about it a lot. Devotions. Quiet time. Prayer journals. We promote these things religiously (pun intended). We have turned the concept of daily time with God into a product often called Quiet Time, and in the process, we've lost the spirit of the thing. Remember, God looks at our hearts. He gauges our attitude. He looks for people who follow the spirit of the law, not just the letter of the law.

The letter of the law says, *Daily quiet times*

. continued next page

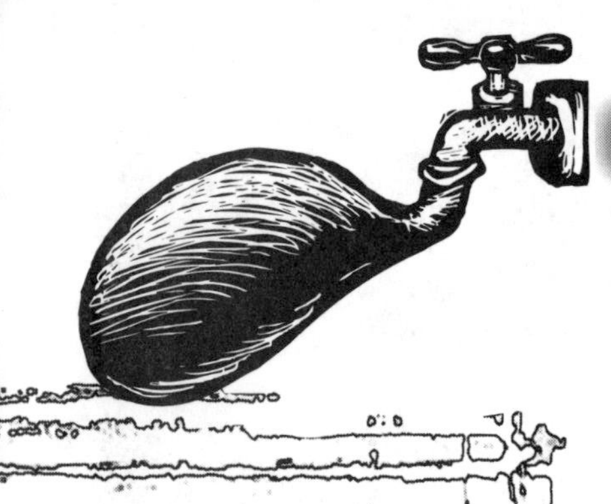

Stepping Back *(cont.)*

are a must. Daily quiet times are a requirement. People who don't have daily quiet times are not worthy to be called children of God.

The spirit of the law says, *With a God like ours, who wouldn't want to spend time with him each day? With a God like ours, no one has to make me spend time with him because I'm continually hungry and thirsty for him. With a God like ours, I simply can't imagine not meeting up with him at every possible chance just to say, "I love you. Thank you."*

The point of studying the psalms in these lessons is not to scare your students into spending time with God daily. The point of studying these psalms is to give them yet another glimpse of the loving God, to expose them to his word, to provide them with an opportunity to hear the truth.

God's love, God's word, and God's truth are the only things you need to show your students...over and over and over again.

▶▶▶Opener (game option) ▶▶▶▶▶▶▶▶▶▶▶▶▶▶▶▶▶▶▶

Water balloon obstacle course

You'll need...
- a dark colored bed sheet
- water balloons
- a large tarp or room with tile floor

When everyone has arrived, open your lesson like this—

Following God—being a Christian—is hard. We have to make right decisions, choose our words carefully, and watch where we step. I want to show you what being a Christian is sometimes like.

Recruit a few volunteers and ask them to leave the room. Send an adult with them. Then place several water balloons on the floor in an area no larger than the size of your bed sheet. Once you've placed the balloons, have four students each hold one corner of the sheet just above the water balloons. When you're ready ask one of the volunteers who's been outside the room to enter. Instruct the student to walk the length of the sheet without popping any water balloons—which, if it's been set up correctly, they shouldn't be able to see.

When the student has reached the end of the sheet, replace balloons as needed and have another volunteer try. When all of your volunteers have walked the length of the sheet, have students gather in the center of the meeting room. Ask questions such as—

- **Compare this experience to your walk with God. How are the two alike?**
- **When has your relationship with God felt like a minefield?**
- **How do you avoid stepping in the wrong places in your everyday life?**

▶▶▶Opener (writing option) ▶▶▶▶▶▶▶▶▶▶▶▶▶▶▶▶▶▶▶

Self-evaluation

You'll need...
- butcher paper or poster board
- markers
- tape or tacks to hang signs

Before students arrive write the following phrases on butcher paper or poster board and hang them in different places in your meeting room.

- I HAVE AN AWESOME, ACTIVE RELATIONSHIP WITH GOD.
- I READ MY BIBLE FREQUENTLY.
- I TRY TO SPEND TIME WITH GOD EVERY DAY.
- I PRAY WHEN I NEED GOD'S HELP OR ADVICE.
- I SPEND TIME WITH GOD WHEN I'M AT CHURCH.

When students arrive, start with something like this—

Today we're going to talk about our relationships with God. I'd like you to go to the sign that best describes your relationship

with God right now. Once you're there I'd like you to think about the results of this type of relationship.

Give students a minute to think, then ask a few volunteers from each sign to share their ideas. Next, have students go to the sign that least describes their relationship with God. When students have found their signs, ask them to think about the results of that kind of relationship, which will be the opposite of what the sign says. For example, if "reading my Bible frequently" least describes a person's relationship, then they should think of the results of a life for a person who doesn't read the Bible frequently. Ask a few students to share their thoughts with the group. Then ask the following question—

- **What one thing hinders your relationship with God the most?**

Conclude either of these openers by saying something like—

Having a daily walk with God is important. It's something God desires. And it's something he hopes we'll desire as well. But as we try to walk with God, things compete with that relationship.

Opener (reflective option)

God and you

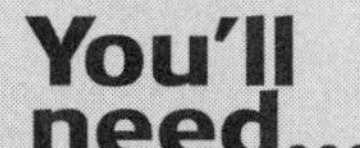

- paper
- pencils

Divide students into groups of four. Begin by saying something like this—

It's not always easy to have an active, vibrant relationship with God. I'd like you to think for a minute about all the things you do—or try to do—to keep your relationship with God close. Make a list of those things.

Give groups several minutes to make their lists. When they're finished have them trade lists with another group. After they have the new list, ask them to rank the things on the list in order of importance with "1" being the most important.

Transition to the next step with words like these—

These lists can help us see that it takes many things to have a strong relationship with God. Though some might seem more important than others, they all are vital if we want to grow in our faith.

You'll need...
- copies of **Baby Steps** (page 37)
- Bibles

▶▶▶In the Book▶▶▶

Baby steps

Divide students into groups of four. Hand out copies of **Baby Steps** (page 37). Then say something like—

> **Sometimes when we talk about living as a Christian, we use the phrase *the Christian walk or walking in God's ways. The psalms say that people who walk in God's ways are blessed. We're going to see what else the psalms say about those who are blessed.***

Give students time to look up the verses and fill in the sheet. Ask a few volunteers to share their answers. Then ask the following questions—

- **Do you feel blessed by God? Explain.**
- **Is walking with God more about our actions or our attitudes? Explain.**
- **Is being blessed more about exterior circumstances or interior attitude? Explain.**
- **One of the verses talked about fearing God. What do you think that means?**

You'll need...
- copies of **Follow the Leader** (page 38)
- Bibles

▶▶▶What it all means (small-group discussion option)▶▶▶

Follow the leader

Have groups of four or five students discuss the questions on **Follow the Leader** (page 38). Allow plenty of time for groups to talk. Then have each group share its responses.

Close the small group session by saying something like this—

> **There's a cycle that keeps our faith strong and healthy. When we spend time with God, say, by reading this psalm, we increase our understanding of the benefits of walking with God. When we understand those benefits we feel blessed ourselves, which prompts us to want to spend more time with God.**

Walking straight, growing strong

Read Psalm 1 aloud. Explain to students that living blessed lives—walking with God—has some clear characteristics. Begin with something like—

> **The psalmist describes walking with God by first explaining what it *isn't*.** [Read verse 1] **If we are following the advice of people who don't believe in or follow God, then we aren't following God. You can't do both. It's either the world's way or God's way. There are only two kinds of people in the world—those who follow God and those who don't. Take a minute and think about which of those two groups you belong to.**

Give kids a few moments to think about which group of people they belong to. Then continue—

> **Then the psalmist goes on to describe what walking with God *is*.** [Read verse 2.] **Walking with God is delighting in God's word, meditating on it, and living it. Sometimes we make Christianity so complicated when in fact it's very simple. If we want to walk with God, we need to get to know him, we need to learn what he says about life, we need to spend time thinking about those things, and then we need to do them. The way we do that is by (1) reading the Bible, his word to us; (2) praying, his communication with us; and (3) obeying his commands, his expectation for us.**
>
> **Think about the relationship you have with your best friend. In your minds make a list of all the things that make that relationship good and strong.**

Give students a few moments to think about this, then continue with—

> **Finally, the psalmist describes the results of walking with God.** [Read verse 3.] **If a tree is planted by a stream, then it will get all the nourishment it needs. Without any effort on its own part—just by letting its roots soak up the water and letting its leaves soak up the sun—the tree will grow, will produce fruit, and will be healthy.**
>
> **It's the same way with a baby. If a baby is fed and nourished, it will grow into a strong and healthy person.**
>
> **That's what our relationship with God is like. If we soak up God's word—if we nourish ourselves—*we will grow*. We will be healthy Christians whose lives produce things that please God. We can't just eat when we feel like it, and we can't just eat whatever we want. We need to eat healthy food and get nourished through the Bible, prayer, and fellowship on a regular basis.**

You'll need...
- copies of **Walk This Way** (page 39)
- pencils

Walk this way

Wind down this lesson by saying something like—

> **We've talked a lot about what it means to be blessed and to walk with God. One of the things that happens when we walk with God is that we begin to recognize all the things he's created and done for us. We begin to appreciate his blessings. I'm going to read you a psalm written by someone who was amazed by God's blessings.**

Read Psalm 65 to your students. After reading it, hand out copies of **Walk This Way** (page 39) and pencils. Give students a few minutes to fill the page out, then close with prayer.

> **Dear God, we want to live our lives for you. We want to walk in your ways so that we can recognize and appreciate all of your blessings. We want to grow in our faith so that our lives please you and produce things that are godly. We want to be like a tree planted by streams of water. We love you. Amen.**

Baby Steps

Look up the verses inside each footprint. Write how each verse describes people who are blessed.

Psalm 1:1

Psalm 32:1

Psalm 128:1

Psalm 40:4

Psalm 41:1

Psalm 112:1

Psalm 65:4

Psalm 89:15

FOLLOW THE LEADER PSALM 1

Before reading this psalm, discuss—

- What does it mean to "walk in God's ways"?
- Why does God want us to follow him?
- When is it most important to follow God?

Read Psalm 128.

Verse 1

- What does it mean to "walk in the counsel of the wicked"?
- What does it mean to "stand in the way of sinners"?
- What do you think "blessed" means?

Verse 2

- What does it mean to be delighted with something?
- How can a person meditate on God's law day and night?

Verse 3

- Think of some of the benefits that a healthy tree offers to people. What are some of the benefits that a healthy Christian can offer to people?

Verses 4-6

- Based on these verses, what are two main differences between those who walk in God's way and the wicked?

When you're finished, discuss—

- What are some ways we can follow God?
- What are some things we can do to get in touch with God?
- How can we encourage others to follow God?
- What are some things that prevent us from walking with God?

Walk This Way

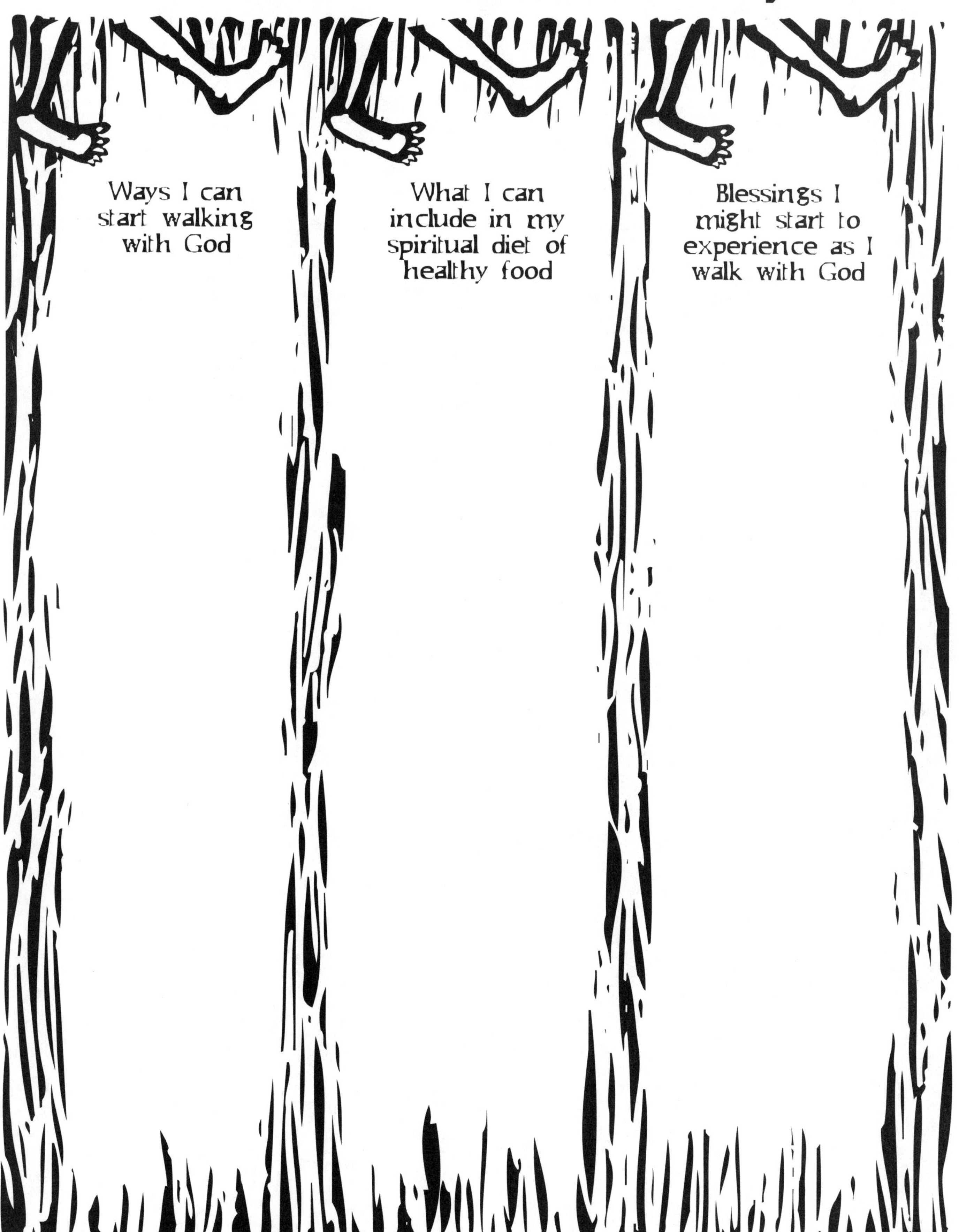

When you're attacked, is God always your bulletproof vest?

Psalm 69

Complaint Psalms

The complaint psalms—those poems of doom and gloom—are usually prayers of either an individual or a community in distress. And we mean *in distress.* Some of the most descriptive metaphors in the book of Psalms are found in these anguished cries—*The waters have come up to my neck...The floods engulf me...I have become like broken pottery...my heart has turned to wax*—there's no doubt about the psalmist's feelings. He's hit rock bottom, and he wants God to know about it.

Check out some other individual complaint psalms. Try Psalms 31, 44, and 140.

Complaint psalms all have certain consistent features—

- Address and appeal—*"Save me, O God."*
- Description of distress—*"I sink in the miry depths...I have come into the deep waters..."*
- Complaint against God—*"My eyes fail looking for my God...I endure scorn for your sake..."*
- Petition—*"Rescue me from the mire...deliver me from those who hate me..."*
- Motivation for God to hear—*"Zeal for your house consumes me..."*
- Accusation against the adversary—*"Many are my enemies without cause..."*
- Call for redress—*"Pour out your wrath on them...Charge them with crime upon crime..."*
- Claims of innocence—*"Those who hate me without reason..."*
- Confessions of sin—*"You know my folly, O God; my guilt is not hidden from you."*
- Professions of trust—*"Answer me with your sure salvation..."*
- Vows to praise for deliverance—*"I will praise God's name in song and glorify him..."*
- Calls to praise—*"Let heaven and earth praise him..."*
- Motivations for praise—*"The Lord hears the needy..."*

(*NIV Study Bible,* introduction to the Psalms)

Stepping Back

Everyone feels attacked by something or someone. The Psalms reassure us that when we're being abused or taking a beating, God is present with us.

Everyone knows what it's like to be beaten up—if not physically, then emotionally.

If you ask the students who fill your youth room, they'll describe a range of feelings they've felt about being attacked. If you ask your kids to describe where God was in the middle of that attack, they may have a difficult time answering. After all, why would a loving God let anyone's life get so rotten and hard to deal with?

Unfortunately, we often spend more energy thinking about the bad times we go through than the good times. When things are good we sail...we coast...we take life for granted. But when things are bad, watch

continued next page

Stepping Back *(cont.)*

out...we whine...we vent...we scream out for someone to sit up and take notice.

Since the Psalms are a collective representation of the joys, sorrows, sins, redemptions, acts, and emotions of real-life people living out their relationship with a sometimes hard-to-understand God, they have something to say to your kids about their bad, gettin'-beat-up, everyone's-out-to-get-me times.

This lesson will help your students gain a deeper understanding of how to tell God about those bad times and how to be assured that he really is there, listening, watching, and loving.

The pattern can shift from one psalm to another, but by looking for the things listed above, it's easy to see that the bottom line is always the same—no matter how bad things may be, no matter how futile things may seem, God will always listen to what we have to say. Things may not get fixed right away, but at least God is aware of the depths of our distress. In the end, the psalmist praises him for that single fact.

Opener (game option)

Protect myself, protect the goods

You'll need...
- Nerf balls
- ong tables
- two bags of candy
- arm bands to distinguish teams (optional)

Before students arrive, set up a Nerf ball attack court in your meeting room. To do this place tables on their sides to serve as hiding places for the kids. Place Nerf balls all around the room.

Have your students form two groups and give each group a bag of candy. Assign areas in the room that the teams are to defend. Have groups hide their candy wherever they want on their side of the room. Instruct kids to form two teams within their groups—one to protect the candy, the other to grab the opposing team's candy. Encourage groups to use the Nerf balls to distract or disable the other team in order to steal its candy.

Say something like—

There are no rules for this game except to do whatever you can to get the other team's candy without hurting anyone in the process.

Allow several minutes for them to try to steal the other team's candy. When time is up, yell, "Stop!" and have both teams get together in the center of the meeting room.

Delve into the lesson by asking some of these questions—

Sometimes life feels like this game—there are no rules except to do whatever it takes to get ahead. But in real life, lots of people can get hurt in the process.

- **How is this game like the times we feel attacked by someone?**
- **When people attack you what do you think they might be after?**
- **Why do you think God allows us to be attacked by people?**
- **When have you felt attacked? What did you do?**

Make the Nerf ball game more, uh, interesting...

- If you've got an outdoor space, consider adding water to your game. Give each group a bucket of water along with the Nerf balls. When the game is over give kids a little time to clean up. Provide towels for kids who are really soaked.

- If you've got more time, make the game more complex by having groups mark the outside of their candy wrappers using a felt tip marker. Then have groups hide their candy anywhere in the church building. Give groups more time to find the other team's candy.

▶▶▶Opener (unfinished-sentence option) ▶▶▶▶▶▶▶▶▶▶▶

You'll need...
- index cards
- pencils
- a basket

I feel attacked when...

As students get into one large circle, open like this—

> **I'd like you to respond to the sentence "I felt attacked when..." Your answer can be serious or funny as long as it's honest and has really happened to you. Don't share your response with anyone and don't write your name on your card. Your answers will remain anonymous.**

Hand out index cards and pencils to all the students. Give them time to think up and write their responses. Have students fold their cards once. Pass a basket around the room for students to drop their cards in.

When the basket returns to you, call up a few students to help you read the cards out loud to the entire group. When you've finished reading all the cards, ask these questions—

- **What did you think about some of the other experiences?**
- **How do you feel when you're being attacked? Explain.**
- **Where do most attacks like these come from?**

Transition to the next section from either of these openers with thoughts like these—

> **Today I'd like to examine what happens to us when we feel attacked. For thousands of years people have experienced times when they felt like others were out to get them. For Christians, who believe that God loves and watches over them, that can be especially hard to understand.**

▶▶▶In the Book ▶▶▶▶▶▶▶▶▶▶▶▶▶▶▶▶▶▶▶▶▶▶▶

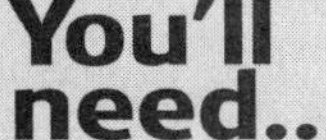

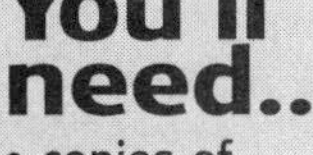

You'll need...
- copies of **Patient Information Sheet** (page 46)
- pencils
- Bibles

The doctor is in

After you've divided your students into groups of four, launch into this section with something like this—

> **For just a few minutes, we're all going to be acting psychologists for someone who's going through a pretty rough time. After reading the patient's complaint, I want you to fill out a Patient Information Sheet.**

Hand out the **Patient Information Sheet** (page 46), pencils, and Bibles to each group. Allow students time to read the psalm and fill in the form. Then gather the groups together to share their observations and to discuss the following questions—

- **What's this person's problem?**
- **Why doesn't God step in and do something?**
- **What would you do if you were in his situation?**

Close by saying something like—

> **It's easy to think that people in the Bible had it easy. But really, they experienced life just like us—including the pain of attack. People like the writer of this psalm learned that it's important to tell God about those times, even if it seems like he's not paying attention.**

You'll need...
- copies of **Where Are You God?** (page 47)
- pencils
- Bibles

▶▶▶What it all means (small-group discussion option)▶▶▶▶

Where are you, God?

Group your students in three or four and distribute **Where Are You God?** (page 47), pencils, and Bibles. Allow plenty of time for the kids to discuss the questions on the sheet. Invite them to share their responses.

End the small group session like this—

> **Sometimes when we're under attack, we feel like we're the only ones experiencing this. We have difficulty understanding where God is. This psalm helps us see that we aren't alone in our struggles.**

You'll need...
- a sign reading ME and one reading THEM
- a length of thin rope or cord
- a pair of scissors

▶▶▶What it all means (leader-talk option)▶▶▶▶▶▶▶▶▶▶▶

It's all *their* fault!

These illustrations can be used as is, or they can be adapted into your own talk.

Begin your talk with something like this—

> **When bad times come we often turn against God and blame him. But the truth is, God sometimes allows us to experience pain so we'll grow. Maybe there's another tough experience coming and God wants us to be prepared for it.**
>
> **When we're besieged we feel like our attackers have control over us.**

To illustrate this point ask two volunteers to come forward. Give one student a sign that reads ME and the other a sign that reads THEM. Tie one end of a piece of rope around "me's" wrist. Have "them" hold the other end of the rope and lead "me" around the room rapidly.

Continue with something like—

There are always going to people who try to control us by ridiculing us. Maybe they don't like our personality. Maybe they're jealous of a skill or talent we have. Maybe the only way they can feel good about themselves is to drag another person down. Maybe they don't like God, so they make fun of our faith. Whatever the reason, it hurts when other people attack us.

The amazing thing about this psalm is that, even though the writer is enduring a lot of pain, he verbally turns to God. While his trust in God doesn't *feel* like it's worth much, the psalmist knows better. And so he relies on what he *knows* even though his feelings don't agree.

While God may not actually stop the attacks or the problems in our lives, he will keep them from overtaking and influencing us if we trust him with it.

Ask "me" and "them" to come forward and begin a mock tug-of-war. As they're doing this hold up a pair of scissors and cut the rope to illustrate what God does for us—sets us free from the power of the attack.

Finish with something like this—

The problem is still there. We can still see it. We can still feel it. And we might still be bothered by it. But God can keep the problem from controlling us, from dragging us down, and from pulling us in different directions. The important thing is to tell him what's going on—honestly—and know that he hears us no matter what we feel.

Closing

When I'm down...

You'll need...
- copies of **When I'm Down** (page 48) for each student
- pencils

Wind down the lesson by saying—

God longs for us to go to him when we're feeling attacked or overwhelmed. He doesn't promise to remove all our problems. But as the psalmist knows, he does listen to us in our pain. Knowing that God is there won't fix all the circumstances in our lives, but it will help us get through them.

Distribute copies of **When I'm Down** (page 48) and pencils to the students. Ask them to fill in the blanks based on what they've learned and talked about. Encourage students to keep the sheets to read later, maybe when they're going through a rough time, as a reminder of what they've learned.

When everyone has had time to finish, close in prayer.

Patient Information Sheet

Read Psalm 69 and fill out this information sheet about the psalmist.

Patient Information

Problem

Symptoms

Diagnosis

Treatment Plan

WHERE ARE YOU, GOD?

Before reading this psalm—

- Talk about a time you felt attacked by a friend. What did you do? How did the problem get resolved?
- Where do you think God is when you're being attacked?
- How does God feel when we're being attacked?

Read Psalm 69.

Verses 1-12

- What are the sources of personal attacks?
- Why do people attack us?
- When have you had the same emotions that the psalmist writes about?
- What scorn have you endured?

Verses 13-18

- What do these verses say about God's presence when we're being attacked?
- What's your first reaction when you feel attacked? Pray? Fight?

Verses 19-21

- Do you believe that God knows about your pain? Explain.
- How can it be that God understands your pain? Explain.

Verses 22-29

- Is it wrong to feel angry towards those who hurt us? Is it wrong to act on that anger? Explain.
- Is it okay to express our anger to God? Explain.

Verses 30-36

- Describe what the psalmist is communicating in these verses.
- Why is it hard to praise God when you're under attack?
- What's the best way to respond to God when you feel beaten up by others?
- When have you been able to praise God when you're being attacked?

After reading this psalm, discuss—

- What does this psalm say about God's presence when we're suffering?
- What does this psalm say about God's help when we're suffering?

When I'm Down

Think about a time when you've felt attacked by other people or circumstances. It could be in the past or it could be right now. Fill in the blanks below telling God how you felt or feel.
O God, I need you! (tell God what's happening)
O God, I can't take it anymore! (tell God how you feel)
O God, please save me! (tell God what you want him to do for you)
O God, I love you! (tell God about your love for him, even when life is tough)

Jesus in the Psalms **Psalms 2 and 110**

Royal Psalms

For years, Israel wanted just one thing from God—an earthly king. They didn't care that God was already their king or that he was watching over them. They wanted a human being they could see, touch, bow down to. And so when God finally granted their desire and established the monarchy, the people had some very strong emotions and reactions. Those are reflected in the royal psalms.

The royal psalms were written for a variety of reasons—to honor a king, to celebrate a coronation, to proclaim the king's mighty deeds, and more. But when we read these royal psalms today, some of them seem to be speaking of Christ. In fact Christ himself often quoted the royal psalms and implied that they'd been written about him.

Psalms has never been considered a prophetic book. Yet in a roundabout way, it does speak of Jesus in its words about the anticipated Messiah. Many royal psalms were written with the knowledge that David's lineage would someday provide a Messiah-king. The Israelites expected this Messiah to be the ultimate earthly king—powerful, strong, and conquering—just like David. Ironically, though, they wrote about the Messiah and described him accurately, they completely missed his arrival.

Jesus didn't conquer in the way they expected. He didn't rule in the way they expected. The most accurate descriptions in the psalms of Jesus' earthly life are the ones of him suffering at the hands of his enemies. And yet we know that the proclamations of his power and lordship and rule are just as accurate even though Jesus never sat on an earthly throne, wielded an earthly scepter, or wore an earthly crown. Jesus turned out to be exactly who the psalmist thought he would be—the ultimate, final, powerful, ruling authority of all creation—packaged in the most humble of all human beings.

Interested in other royal-type psalms? Read Psalms 20, 45, 72, or 99.

Stepping Back

The royal psalms remind us of the divine royalty of Jesus. They give us a glimpse of who he was promised to be, long before he was ever born into this world.

Jesus in the Psalms? It's probably not something you think about too much. You already know that there's a ton of information about Jesus and a lot of prophecy about him way before John the Baptist said one word. But how much of this information do your *students* know?

Some teens may already realize that Jesus is mentioned or referred to throughout the Old Testament. Others have no clue. This lesson will help your students get a grip on Jesus' presence in the Old Testament. But it offers them much more.

Reminding your students how the Old Testament foretold the coming of Jesus years before his birth gives them a bigger

- continued next page

Stepping Back *(cont.)*

picture of the existence and power of Jesus. So what if they already know that Jesus is powerful—learning more about this helps them begin to grasp how big God really is.

Try to get your kids to step inside the wonder of the people who actually met Jesus when he walked the earth. Imagine expecting the Messiah in a cloud and then actually getting him in a manger. This is a struggle your students need to see.

A well-rounded understanding of the Old Testament Jesus will help your students understand the type of ruler and Messiah that the early Jews felt they needed. They didn't want someone warm and fuzzy. They wanted someone who was powerful, strong, decisive, and stoic. The writers of the royal psalms clearly expected someone who would offer instant relief from suffering.

Christians know that Jesus is everything the Old Testament prophets and the writers of the royal psalms said he would be—he is powerful, he is awesome, he has conquered the ultimate enemy in death, he rules the world, he is in control. It's good for our students to be reminded that Jesus is not just their best friend and close bud—he's also the God of the universe.

Opener [writing/presentation option]

Expectant parents

You'll need...
- paper
- pencils

Lead into the lesson with words like these—

Today I'd like you to imagine that you're expectant parents. Your baby is due any day now, and you've decided to write a speech about your child—what you expect of her, what you think she'll become, what you hope she'll accomplish, what you want her to stand for. Be creative.

Pair students up—guy-guy and girl-girl is best unless your students are really comfortable together. When pairs have finished writing their speeches, have them present to the group. Encourage discussion with some questions like—

Perhaps you have students who *are* expecting-or already have children. Have them write about their own children, not imaginary ones. This has potential for being a profound experience. But, as always, use your own judgment about the appropriateness of the activity for your group.

- **If you were really expecting a baby, what things do you think you might want to know?**
- **Is it okay to make decisions about your life based on what you think your baby will be like? Explain.**
- **How do you think parents feel when their child doesn't become the person they'd hoped or expected?**

Opener [creative option]

Ad campaigns

You'll need...
- five pillowcases
- a roll of toilet paper, a box of tissue, a sponge, a bar of soap, a box of cereal
- tacks to hang pillowcases on the wall
- paper
- pencils

Prior to your kids' arrival, hang the pillowcases (with the objects already inside) on the walls of your meeting room. *Be sure the objects aren't visible through the pillowcases.* To begin say something like—

Today we're going to create marketing campaigns for some new products that will be out soon. It will be your job to sell the product based on how great it is, what it has to offer, and why a person simply has to have it.

Divide students into five groups (or however many pillowcases you use.) Distribute paper and pencils. Send one group to each pillowcase. Instruct them to *look at* the pillowcase but to *not touch* it. Based on what they see, they should guess what the object is.

Instruct them to come up with their best sales pitch based on what they think is inside. Allow plenty of time for creative brainstorming, and then have each group present its sales pitch. After each presentation have the group bring out its object to see how accurate its assumptions were. Bring home the point by asking some questions—

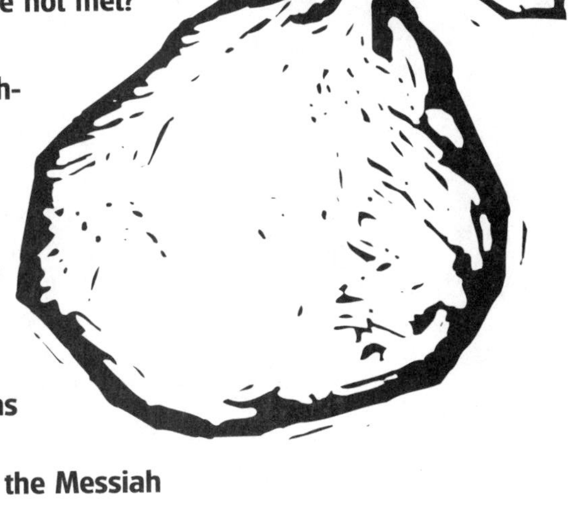

- **What's the difference between assuming you know something and actually knowing it?**
- **When have you had expectations that were not met? How did that feel?**
- **How difficult is it to predict something without having all the facts?**

Close either of these openers by saying something like—

It can be difficult to totally understand something without seeing it or touching it. Today we're going to look at how the Psalms portray Jesus. We're going to see that the psalmists had a very strong opinion of who the Messiah would be and how he would conquer the earth.

In the Book

You'll need...
- copies of **Who Is Jesus?** (page 55)
- pencils
- Bibles

Breaking news

Start this section like this—

Meeting Jesus would be an amazing thing. I'd like you to take a look at some psalms written by people who hoped to one day meet Jesus. Their descriptions were based on how they thought a Messiah-king should look and act.

Divvy your students up into two groups and pass around copies of **Who Is Jesus?** (page 55). Ask them to read each psalm and respond by writing character traits or descriptions of Jesus based on what they read.

When they're finished say something like—

Jesus was spoken about long before his appearance on earth. Since he was God, people were expecting that he'd be some amazing king who conquered evil and ruled the world. I'd like you to look at who Jesus was when he actually walked the earth to see how accurate this picture was.

You'll need...
- copies of **Snapshots of Jesus** (page 56)
- pencils
- Bibles

▶▶▶What it all means (Bible-study option) ▶▶▶▶▶▶▶▶▶▶

Snapshots of Jesus

Group students into threes or fours and open with this type of comment—

You've seen what the psalmists expected of Jesus. Now I'd like you to take a look at the reality of Jesus on earth.

Pass out pencils and copies of **Snapshots of Jesus** (page 56). Tell students to read each passage and then write a description of Jesus based on what they read. Allow about 10 minutes. Break groups apart and have everyone pair up with a student from another group to share their snapshot descriptions. Ask for volunteers to share their descriptions with the group. Then ask—

- **Based on what you've seen here, who was Jesus?**
- **How closely do your snapshots of Jesus match up with the psalmist's expectations for the Messiah-king?**
- **What have you learned about Jesus from these snapshots that you didn't know before?**
- **If you met the person that your snapshot pictures describe, but you were expecting him to be strong and powerful and kingly, what would your reaction be?**

Jesus wasn't just a character mentioned briefly in the Psalms. He was a greatly anticipated living, breathing human being. And while he wasn't the conquering king that these psalms suggested he would be, he did come to save us.

You'll need...
- copies of **Discovering Jesus** (page 57)
- Bibles

▶▶▶What it all means (small-group discussion option) ▶▶▶▶

Discovering Jesus

Distribute copies of **Discovering Jesus** (page 57) to students in groups of about four. Instruct them to discuss the questions on the sheet. If there's time, you can discuss some of the questions as a large group.

Close the small group session by saying something like—

It's clear from the Psalms that people expected Jesus to appear as a powerful, conquering king, but they got something entirely different. The real Jesus behaved nothing like the psalmists' descriptions. But however he acted, Jesus' purpose was clear—he came to save us.

▶▶▶What it all means (leader-talk option) ▶▶▶▶▶▶▶▶▶▶

The roles Jesus played

You'll need...
- a roll of aluminum foil

Hold up a piece of aluminum foil and explain to students that you're going to use it to illustrate the different pictures of Jesus in the Bible. Begin with—

> **Who Jesus Was**
>
> **The Old Testament reveals what most people from that time era expected Jesus to be. For a completely *different* picture, however, listen to the words of Isaiah.**

Read Isaiah 53:1-5. Ask a volunteer to come forward, then press the aluminum foil onto his face to make an impression. Show students the impression and explain that this is just one way to see the foil. Continue with—

> **Who Jesus Became**
>
> **How Jesus actually entered the worldly scene, however, is still *another* picture of the Messiah. In Luke 2:1-20 we read about no conquering general, no beat-up victim, but about the birth of a child to a first-century working-class couple.**

Read the Luke passage to your students. Ask another volunteer to come forward and press the foil to her face. Display this new impression to your students. Point out that you're using the same foil, but a totally different impression was formed. Continue with—

> **There were many different ideas of who Jesus would be. They were all true—but varied views—of Jesus.**
>
> **Who Jesus Is**
>
> **We can look all day at Jesus in the Bible—at the things he's done and the things people expected him to be. There are thousands of books that talk about Jesus. Eventually, though, we've got to look at who Jesus is in our own lives. Knowing a lot of information about Jesus is great, but if that information doesn't make it to our hearts, then it's useless.**

▶▶▶Closing ▶▶▶▶▶▶▶▶▶▶▶▶▶▶▶▶▶▶▶▶▶▶▶▶▶▶▶▶

The Jesus I Know

You'll need...
- copies of **The Jesus I Know** (page 58)
- pencils

Hand out copies of **The Jesus I Know** (page 58) and pencils to each student. Explain to them that Jesus is many different things to many different people, depending on their experiences, their level of trust, how long they've had a relationship with him, and what they've been taught. Ask students to take a few minutes to think about Jesus and the things they know about him.

Have them write those things on the sheet. They can be single words, short phrases, or sentences. After a few minutes, close in a prayer like this—

> **Dear God, thank you for sending Jesus to earth so we could know you. Thank you that he died and rose again so we could have a relationship with you. We want to know Jesus more and more each day. Show us who he is more clearly so that we can become more like him. Amen.**

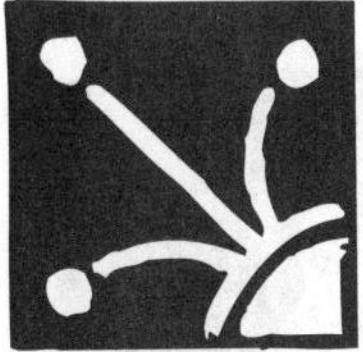 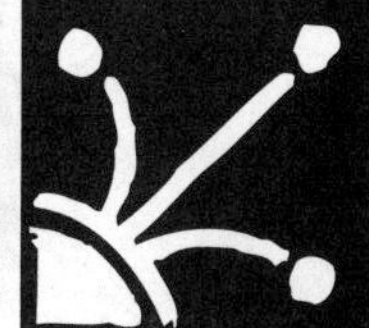 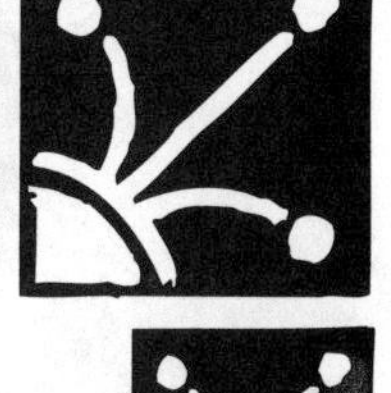

WHO IS JESUS?

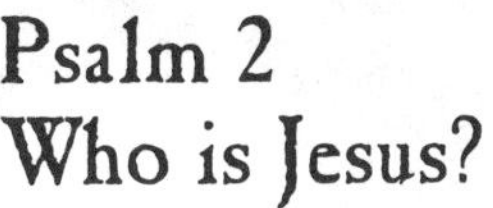

Psalm 2
Who is Jesus?

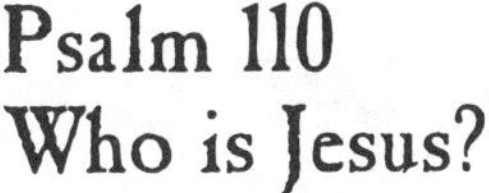

Psalm 110
Who is Jesus?

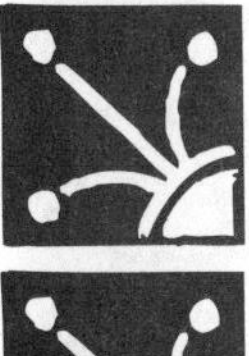 

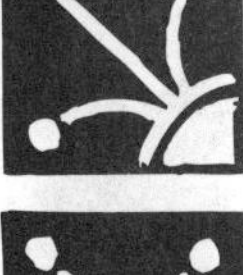 

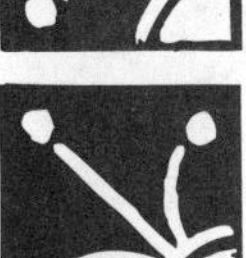 

SNAPSHOTS OF JESUS
Look up the following Scripture references, and write a description of Jesus based on each passage.
Snapshot
Matthew 27:31-50
Snapshot
Mark 2:6-11
Snapshot
John 1:1-14
Snapshot
Luke 12:49-53

DISCOVERING JESUS Psalms 2 and 110

Before reading these psalms—
- What do you think Jesus was doing when people were living through Old Testament times?

Read Psalm 2.
Verses 1-4
- In your opinion, what individuals, groups, or organizations overtly oppose Jesus?
- What does *conspire* mean? Why do people conspire against Jesus?

Verses 5-9
- What do these verses say about Jesus?
- Why do these passages describe Jesus as smashing things?

Verses 10-12
- What does it mean to *kiss the Son?*
- What does it mean to *take refuge* in him?

Read Psalm 110.
Verse 1
- The first line says, "The Lord says to my Lord." What do you think that means?
- What does it mean that God makes our enemies a footstool?

Verses 2-7
- What picture of Jesus do you get from these verses?
- Why does this psalm use strong military language?

After reading these psalms—
- Describe the picture of Jesus these psalms portray.
- Talk about a time when you experienced Jesus like these psalms describe.
- Discuss some things that you learned from reading these psalms.

The Jesus I Know

Write down all the things you know about him.

The God who really knows you, inside and out **Psalm 139**

Trust Psalms

Remember the chorus from the old hymn "Trust and Obey"?

> *Trust and obey, for there's no other way*
> *To be happy in Jesus, but to trust and obey.*

It's a simple chorus with a very simple truth—the only way to have a fulfilling relationship with Jesus is to trust him. Completely.

Trust psalms convey that same simple message. They describe a confident, blind, even alarming trust in God. Such a deep and simple level of trust inevitably produces intimacy. And intimacy, in turn, feeds the trust. They are mutually inclusive. Anyone who's ever been in a close relationship knows that.

Check out Psalms 11, 16, 23, 28, and 62 for a few more samples.

Psalm 139 is a beautiful and familiar example of a trust psalm. Certain parts of it are familiar to all of us. But it's also a beautiful example of the main stylistic feature of Hebrew poetry—parallel lines. Rather than rhyming poetry, the psalms are poems that repeat the same idea in two different ways.

> *Where can I go from your spirit?*
> *Where can I flee from your presence?*

Or—

> *You discern my going out and my lying down;*
> *You are familiar with all my ways.*

Or—

> *Search me, O God, and know my heart;*
> *Test me and know my anxious thoughts.*

By following this writing style, the psalmists hit upon a great idea—sometimes saying the same thing in a new and different way helps more peo-

Stepping Back

God makes us. God searches us. God knows us. And he wants us to seek out and know him, too, so we can have an intimate relationship with him.

Sit back for a moment and ponder—which of these scenarios do you relate to most?

- **"Hey, Mac. How's that devotional life going?"**
- **"I'd like to know more about you, Phylicia. Why don't you tell me one of your deep, dark secrets that no one else knows.**
- **"Could you pass the chips, hon? By the way, happy anniversary!"**
- **You to yourself: "I wish someone cared enough to ask me what I'm going through right now."**

These statements all reflect varying levels of trust and intimacy between two people. Which one describes *your* level of comfort with oth-

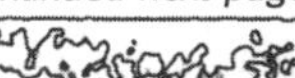

-continued next page

ple grasp the concept. This trust psalm demonstrates it clearly.

The poetry is beautiful. The message of trust is simple. The concept of intimacy is profound. And all of those are available to us today when we take the time to read this psalm and revel in the writer's rich relationship with God.

Stepping Back *(cont.)*

ers? Now ask yourself how intimate you are with God. What are you intimate enough to ask of him? How willing are you to hear the truth from him?

Ponder the students in your youth ministry for a moment. Do you sense that they're intimate with God? Do you think they regularly sit down with him and say, "Hey God, could you take a few minutes to check out my heart and mind, and then let me know what you think?"

In today's world, where exterior image matters more than interior character, your students are probably crying out for someone to know them—*really* know them, on the inside, where it matters. Use this psalm to help your students learn how to open up to God and start to know him intimately.

Opener (game option)

Manhunt

You'll need...
- **Manhunt** worksheet prepared ahead of time (see below) for each student
- pencils

Before this lesson gather information about your students that you can use in a scavenger hunt-like activity. You can use birthrates, number of siblings, ethnic heritage, birthplaces, or any other personal-individual information. Use the data you gather to create a list that kids must fill in. For example—

- Who was born in Nebraska?
- Who has grandparents from Ecuador?
- Who was born on May 17, 1985?

Make your list between 15 and 20 questions. Make enough copies for your entire group.

Start the hunt with something like this—

Tonight you're going on a manhunt. In your hands you have a list of facts about people in this room. It's your job to find out who they are. It's as easy as going up to someone and saying, [use one of your questions as an example]**. You have five minutes to get as many answers as you can.**

Explain to students that they can only ask specific questions—for example, "Were you born on May 17, 1985" instead of, "Are you one of the people on this sheet and if so, which one?" Also, the people who are answers to the Manhunt questions should not volunteer that information to anyone who doesn't ask them specifically—so it's not okay to go up to their friends and say, "Hey, I'm the answer to number 3."

When time's up call everyone back together and ask them the following questions—

- **How was your quest like the way you search for something important?**
- **How was this similar to the way God looks for us?**
- **How was this similar to the way we look for God?**
- **Have you ever set yourself on a quest for something (or someone)?**
- **How did you go about accomplishing that?**

Close this opener by saying something like—

God is on a quest for us—specifically, a quest for our trust and our intimacy. And he won't be satisfied until he gets it.

Today we're going to talk about God's desire to search every corner of who we are—and *why* God wants to do this.

▶▶▶Opener (large-group option) ▶▶▶▶▶▶▶▶▶▶▶▶▶▶▶▶

Trust fall

You'll need...
- blank paper
- markers

This is an old group-growing game that'll help your kids grasp the concept of trusting God.

Have your students gather in one circle. The circle needs to be small enough so that a person in the middle can easily be caught. Recruit a volunteer to stand in the center with arms crossed on her chest. If you have a large group you can break into several groups with a volunteer for each circle. Ask the students in the circle to stand shoulder to shoulder with their arms held out in front of them, palms up, ready to catch. The volunteer should let herself fall without bending at the knees or waist, against the other students' hands. Instruct the students supporting the volunteer to gently pass her around the circle.

Next ask a different volunteer to stand on the edge of a chair. Line the other students up shoulder to shoulder in two lines, facing each other. Students should grab the arms of the person across from them. Direct the volunteer to cross his arms across his chest and fall backward into the arms of the students behind him. When several volunteers have taken a turn, ask the following questions—

- **How is this exercise like trusting God?**
- **When have you had difficulty trusting God?**
- **What is it difficult to trust God for?**

Transition into the next section like this—

It takes a lot of trust to let someone know us, even if that someone is God. Let's begin by looking at a passage from the Bible where one person had an unbelievable trust in God and a deep desire for intimacy with him.

▶▶▶In the Book ▶▶▶▶▶▶▶▶▶▶▶▶▶▶▶▶▶▶▶▶▶▶▶▶

Search me, O God

You'll need...
- soft instrumental music
- tape or CD player
- copy of Psalm 139 from the *NIV*, *The Message*, and the *New Living Translation* (or your choice of translations)

Have students find a place where they can be somewhat alone and comfortable, either in chairs or laying on the floor, and say something like this—

We don't often have time to just sit and listen to what the Bible says. One of the ways we begin to trust and know someone intimately, though, is by spending time with them. *Lots* of time. I

A good song to use during this lesson is "I Am," by Jill Phillips from the *WOW 2000* CD.

want you to close your eyes, relax, and listen to the words of Psalm 139 while I read them to you. Maybe as you listen you can make the psalmist's words your own.

Play the instrumental music softly while reading the Psalm from at least two different versions of the Bible. If you prefer, ask another leader or a student. Be sure to read slowly so kids have a chance to absorb what's being read. When you've finished say something like this—

What this psalmist was asking is incredible. Remember, this person was asking a God whom he had never seen to invade him, to search out both the good and the bad things. Obviously, he trusted God deeply. We may not have many people we can trust like that. But God is waiting and wanting that kind of relationship with you. And he's worthy of our trust.

What it all means (small-group discussion option)

God's searchlight

You'll need...
- copies of **God's Searchlight** (page 65)
- Bibles

Have students gather in groups of four and distribute copies of **God's Searchlight** (page 65) and Bibles to each group. Allow plenty of time for discussion, then invite everyone back to the large group to share responses.

Close the small group session by saying something like—

God's not just sitting there in heaven watching us. He's working in us, examining us, looking for things that hinder our relationship with him. The psalmist is expressing his desire to be searched. God longs to look us over as well.

What it all means (leader-talk option)

Look me over, God

Begin your talk with something like this—

Not all of us are like the psalmist in the passage we just studied. Opening up to God and asking him to examine us isn't easy for most of us, but I think I've got some ideas that might help us begin opening up to God.

If you want to read Psalm 139 to your students again, do it now. If you think it's still fresh in their minds from the earlier activity, go on with the talk.

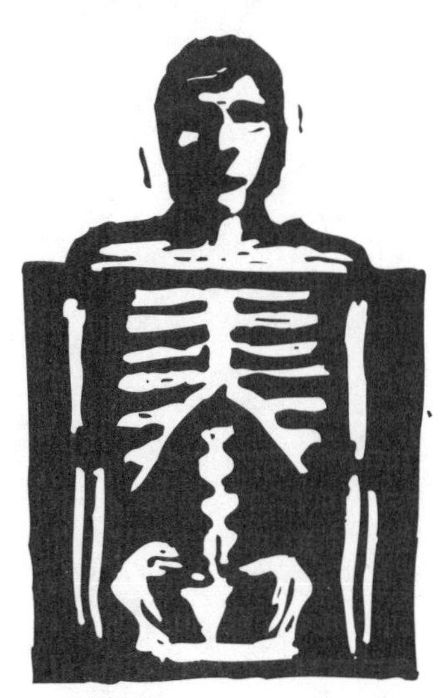

An important first step in letting God examine us is stopping long enough to let him take a look. How should we stop? How should we let God look us over?

Stopping involves three things—taking time, finding a quiet place, and focusing on God. Then we've got to ask God to examine us. That's as simple as saying, "God, please take a look at me." You might even want to say what the psalmist said, 'Search me, O God, and know my heart."

Ask students to spend a few seconds thinking about when and how they might find time to focus on God. Continue with—

Once we've asked God to look us over, two things might happen. First, we might actually sense God's presence and feel closer to him. But second, we'll probably realize there are some things in our lives he wants to get rid of. It might be sin,, or it might be something that we value too much. Things that keep us from spending time with God and growing closer to him should go. We have a choice at this point. We can either ignore God and pretend there's nothing in our lives he might want to change or we can say, "Here it is," and give it to God.

Ask students to spend a few seconds thinking about what God might find if they actually ask him to search their hearts. Continue with—

We've got to get rid of whatever prevents us from growing closer to God. That's not easy to do because it's probably something we value—otherwise it wouldn't be in our lives in the first place. The question is this: what do we value more—our relationship with God or the thing that is keeping us from knowing God better?

Ask students to spend a few seconds thinking about what is most valuable to them—their relationship with God or the other things that fill their lives.

Closing (writing activity)

You'll need...
- copies of **Here I Am** (page 66) for each student
- pencils

Here I am

Lead into this time with words like these—

God's waiting to know us. He's longing to search every part of us, to find the things that are keeping us from knowing him more intimately, and to get rid of those things so we can become closer to him. Let's spend a few minutes thinking about the parts of our lives that we've never let God examine.

Give each student a copy of **Here I Am** (page 66) and a pencil. Encourage students to fill out the sheet like the psalmist might have. Remember the parallel lines in Hebrew poetry mentioned at the beginning of this lesson? That's what you want to help your students accomplish here. Give them some of these examples if you think they're struggling with this activity.

Under *Here I am* they might write, *I'm seeking you, God...I want to know you...I'm listening to you.*

Under *Here it is* they might write, *I'm way too busy...I spend so much time watching TV...I try to read my Bible, but it never seems to happen.*

Under *Take it away* they might write, *I'm going to stop doing so much extra stuff...I'm going to spend time with you each morning...I'm going to try to learn how to hear your voice.*

When they've had a few minutes, close in prayer with words like these—

God, you made each of us. You love each of us. You desire to know each of us deeply and to have us know you in return. We need your help with that. There're so many things that fills our days, and many of them keep us from getting to know you better. Please show us what we need to give up or give to you in order to know you more intimately. Amen.

GOD'S SEARCHLIGHT PSALM 139

Before you read this psalm, discuss—

- When was the last time you sat in silence and asked God to examine your heart? What was that like? What happened?
- Why is letting God examine us important?
- What are the benefits of letting God examine us?
- What are the drawbacks to letting God examine us?

Read Psalm 139.

Verses 1-4

- If God already knows us, why do we need to ask him to search us?
- What does it mean to be completely known by God?
- What is the significance of pointing out things like sitting and rising?

Verses 5-13

- What does it mean to be "hemmed in"?
- Based on what this psalm says, is it possible to escape God's presence? Is it possible to escape God's examination?
- What's the difference between being in God's presence and being examined by God?
- Since God made us, can we prevent him from knowing us? Explain.
- How does God knit us together?

Verses 14-16

- What does it mean to be made with fear?

Verses 17-22

- Based on this passage, are we able to examine God? Explain.
- What does it mean that God's thoughts are uncountable? What does that imply about the time he took to create you?

Verses 23-24

- If God finds something offensive in us, what should we do? What should he do?
- Can we be led into eternity with anything offensive in us?
- Can we know about the things that are offensive in us unless we let God search us?

After you read this psalm—

- Describe the picture you have of God after reading this psalm.
- Describe the picture you think God has of you after reading this psalm.

HERE I AM

Shedding old skin—forgiveness and renewal **Psalm 51**

Penitential Psalms

Penitential psalms are what you sing, say, or even scream when you've sinned big time and you know it. They're not exclusive to the Psalms, but they're brought most notably to the forefront by this one—David's cry for forgiveness and mercy from God after his affair with Bathsheba.

Psalm 51 is one of the seven penitential psalms of early Christian tradition. Chances are you're very familiar with it already. In some ways it's become the poster child for forgiveness exercises in youth ministry. It's also been the source of many recent praise and worship choruses.

The other six penitential psalms of early Christian tradition are 6, 32, 38, 102, 130, and 143.

Obviously it strikes home in the hearts of many believers, in part because it's filled with such descriptive phrases. In verse 7, David says, *"Cleanse me with hyssop, and I will be clean."* The Hebrew word David used for *cleanse* literally means to "un-sin," revealing his eagerness to be completely washed from his sin. And check out David's choice of plants—hyssop. Hyssop was a plant used in the ritual cleansing of persons healed of leprosy, a disease that resulted in being totally outcast and rejected by society. David is asking to have renewed access into God's presence, to no longer be outcast or rejected because of his sin.

When David says, "*Create in me a pure heart,*" he uses the same word used in Genesis when God created the world. God's creative muscle, flexed at the creation of the world, is called upon in this desperate cry from David. David isn't just saying, "Hey, God, clean my heart!" He's say, "Hey, God give me a new heart for you. " David's asking for surgery. He wants God to take out his old heart and give him a new one. (*Interpreter's Bible Commentary,* 269-270).

Maybe the reason Psalm 51 has inspired so many songs and so many forgiveness exercises is because at one time or another, we all feel like David did—we want God to take our sinful hearts and give them a good once over, leaving us with brand new hearts that are totally devoted to him.

Stepping Back

Everyone makes mistakes. The Psalms help us understand that when we blow it, God's right there waiting to forgive us.

Chances are your kids clearly understand the New Testament picture of forgiveness. They've probably got a good handle on what Jesus did for them on the cross. After all, the music we play for them, the talks we give to them, and the pictures we paint for them about their spiritual lives all include messages of repentance and forgiveness based on a New Testament understanding. But have you ever stopped to consider the Old Testament picture of forgiveness? We don't spend much time talking about it, do we?

But consider that without a picture of God's forgiveness in the Old Testament, students get a skewed understanding of God's actions in history. They might possibly think

- continued next page

Stepping Back *(cont.)*

"The Old Testament equals God killing people for the Israelites. The New Testament equals God forgiving people and telling us about heaven."

Draw kids a picture of a God who forgave long before Jesus came to die. Show them that God attempted to redeem his people long before they ever fully realized it.

As you teach this study, remember a few things—

- Some teenagers feel awkward and think they're no good. Consequently they feel that God could never love them, which leads them to embrace sin as a natural thing. The logic goes, "If I'm bad anyway, why not just give up?"
- Some teenagers feel unforgivable. They may think their sin can't be forgiven because it's too big for God to forget.

continued next page

▶▶▶Opener (large-group option)

One bad thing

You'll need...
- index cards
- pencils

When you're ready to begin, give each youth an index card and a pencil. Ask students to think back to when they were in grade school. Have them write down one example of when they broke a rule and the consequences for it. For example, someone might say that in kindergarten she pushed another kid and had to sit in the corner for 15 minutes. Or maybe another called his little sister stupid and so he had to write "I will be nice" 100 times. This should be a truthful but lighthearted activity.

When the cards have been passed in to you, read each one aloud then say something like this—

> **When we were younger, our parents and teachers tried to give us clear rules and guidelines. If we broke them, there were consequences. The consequences usually weren't so much about punishing us as they were about helping us remember the right behavior for the next time. Usually, we're forgiven for what we did and given another chance. As we grow older we have more choices facing us all the time. And sometimes when we break the rules, whether it's our parents', our teachers', or God's rules, we don't get caught so the consequences aren't always as obvious as when we were young. But the sin—the rule-breaking—is still a part of us until we are forgiven for it.**

▶▶▶Opener (small-group option)

Biggest mistake

Assemble students in groups of four and ask them to think of a famous person who made a *big,* well-publicized mistake during the last year or so. For example, students might think of a movie star who's been arrested or a significant political figure who got caught in a scandal. Once groups have chosen a person, have them decide on just punishment for the person's mistake. Groups can be as inventive as they want.

When students are ready give each group the chance to present their situations and punishments. Encourage discussion with the following questions.

- **When have you sinned and tried to hide it?**
- **Does hiding your sin make it go away, or does it still bother you?**
- **When you've gotten away with something—not gotten caught or punished—how do you feel inside?**

Regardless of which opener you choose, transition into the next section like this—

> **Today we're going to talk about something as old as humanity—sin. All of us have done it. And we all need to be forgiven for the wrong things we've done, continue to do, and will do. For centuries people have been seeking God's forgiveness for their bad behavior.**

In the Book

You'll need...
- paper
- pencils
- Bibles

David's sin

Arrange your students in groups of four and have them read 2 Samuel 11:1-17. Ask them to imagine what it might have been like to be David. Distribute paper and pencils for the groups to write out three of the most prevalent emotions that they think David felt in the midst of the sin he was committing. When they're finished, pair groups up to share their ideas.

Continue with the lesson by saying something like—

> **Now that you've read about the huge sin David committed, I'd like you to see how he reacted to it before God.**

Instruct the groups to read Psalm 51 and write down the emotions that David expressed to God in this psalm. Once again, have each group discuss their findings with another group. Invite some volunteers to share their responses with the entire class. Encourage participation with some of these questions—

- **Why did David sin?**
- **What differences do you notice between David's emotions in 2 Samuel and those in Psalm 51?**
- **How do you think God felt about David's sin?**
- **What similarities are there between David's sins and ours?**

Continue with something like—

> **God forgave David, but did you notice how genuinely sorry David was? This is one guy who really wanted God to forgive what he'd done. We're just like David. We all sin and we all need forgiveness.**

Stepping Back *(cont.)*

There are three ways to deal with these emotions.

1. Love—Demonstrate unconditional love for your kids. Don't be shocked by their sin.
2. Acceptance—Kids need to know that you'll have open arms for them before and after they sin.
3. Restitution—Always help kids see the big picture. When students tell you about their sin, be sure to mention how they can find forgiveness and acceptance in Jesus.

Use this lesson to help your students embrace God's loving forgiveness.

You'll need...
- copies of **Have Mercy on Me** (page 72)
- pencils
- Bibles

▶▶▶What it all means (small-group option)▶▶▶▶▶▶▶▶▶▶

Have mercy on me

Give each group of four a copy of **Have Mercy on Me** (page 72). After groups discuss the questions on the sheet, have the entire class come together to share their responses.

Close the small group session by saying something like—

> **Sin separates us from God. It gets in the way of our having a vital, active, thriving relationship with the Creator of the universe. I'd like us to focus on how we can get rid of the things that prevent an intimate relationship with God.**

You'll need...
- a refrigerator box
- markers

▶▶▶What it all means (leader-talk option)▶▶▶▶▶▶▶▶▶▶

Boxed off by sin

If you can't score a refrigerator box, create a barrier using butcher paper or a bed sheet.

Before presenting this talk to students, get a large refrigerator box (available for free at most appliance stores). Place it in the center of the meeting room.

Begin by reading Psalm 51. If you've already studied it, ask students to share what they've learned so far. You might want to give them your impressions and share some things that you've gained from the study. Bring students up to write on the outside of the box a few things that are typical sins for students their age. Have students take their seats, but ask one student to stand inside the box and one to stand outside.

- **Sin prevents our relationship with God from growing.**
  Imagine that the person inside the box has committed one or some or all of the sins written on the outside. The person outside the box is God. Take a close look. Do you think the person inside the box can communicate with the person outside very well? Not with that wall between them. This represents what happens when we continue to live with the sins we've committed. They separate us from God.

Now invite three or four other students to come stand outside the box also. Continue with—

- **Sin prevents our relationships with others from growing.**
  I'ts not just impossible to have a relationship with God when we're living inside our sin. It's also impossible to have a strong relationship with other people. Our sin builds walls between us and God, and it also builds walls between us and other people. It's impossible to have a strong relationship with someone who lives in a box. If we all have unconfessed sin, it's like we're all

living in our own little boxes, shut off from God and shut off from others.

Have all the students return to their seats and end with something like this—

The only way these relationships can be restored is by asking for forgiveness. Then the sin is wiped away, and the walls are torn down. That makes it possible for us to communicate with God and with others the way he intended. We could all benefit by following David's example of heartfelt repentance.

▶▶▶Closing ▶▶▶▶▶▶▶▶▶▶▶▶▶▶▶▶▶▶▶▶▶▶▶▶▶▶▶▶▶

You'll need...

- a laptop computer
- blank paper
- pencils

Wiping out sins

On one table set blank paper and pencils. On another set a laptop computer.

Give students a few moments to think about something they want God to forgive them for. Then give them two options for this section. They can either take paper and pencils and write out their sin—along with some of their emotions and thoughts about it, or they can go to the laptop computer and type their sin. If they write by hand, have them fold up their papers several times. If they use the computer, instruct them to hit the return key until a new page appears so that no one can read what they wrote. They can also hold down the <ctrl> and <alt> keys while hitting <enter> to create a new page instantly.

When all students have finished, gather up the handwritten papers. Then say something like—

Forgiveness is available to us all the time. All we have to do is ask for it. But we have to ask for it with a humble and genuine heart. Remember, God's forgiveness may be free to us, but it cost him his very life. Forgiveness is free, but it is not cheap.

Give your students a visual demonstration of God's forgiveness by taking the handwritten papers and tearing them into small pieces and throwing them away. Then go to the computer, select the entire file, and delete it. Tell your students that God's forgiveness is that quick and that complete. Close in a prayer something like this—

God, we all sin. And we all know it. It's hard to admit the things we've done wrong. We'd rather just pretend they're not there or hope they'll go away on their own. We know our sin keeps us from having the kind of relationship with you that's right. God, please show us our sins and give us the humility to ask for your forgiveness. You promise to forgive any sin if we only ask. We're asking. Thank you for your great promise and for keeping it. Amen.

Have Mercy on Me Psalm 51

Before reading this psalm—

- Describe a time when you knew that you had sinned but weren't willing to admit it.
- Talk about how sin has impacted the life of someone you know. If you don't know someone deeply affected by sin, talk about someone you've heard about.
- Give the group your own definition of sin.

Read Psalm 51.

Verses 1-2

- What makes us candidates for God's mercy?
- Who is allowed to receive God's compassion?
- What things in our life might we need God's mercy for?

Verses 3-6

- What does it mean to be "aware of your sin"?
- What does it mean to sin against the Lord?
- What's the difference between living a life of sin and living a life of truth?
- Describe a time when you were aware of a sin in your life. What happened?

Verses 7-12

- How does God cleanse us?
- Why does God want us clean?
- What do we have to do anything to be cleansed?

Verses 13-19

- Other than being spiritually clean, what are some benefits of God's forgiveness?
- What does it mean to have a broken spirit?
- What does it mean to have a contrite heart?

After reading this psalm, discuss—

- How has your definition of sin changed as a result of this psalm?
- How do you think David felt after writing this psalm?
- If you were God, how would you feel hearing this?

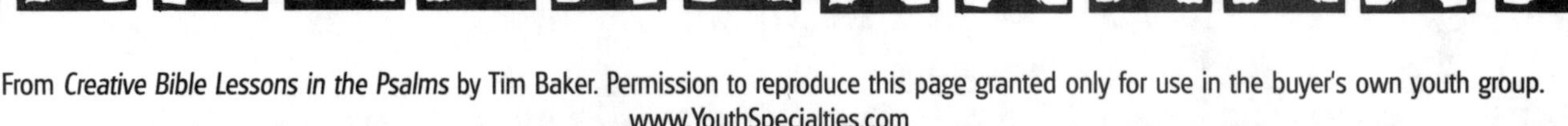

Gratitude is next to godliness **Psalm 118**

Thanksgiving Psalms

Thanksgiving psalms—no, they're not something you recite before eating a turkey in November. These are psalms that grow in you and burst out when you're uncontrollably compelled to thank God for what he's done or is doing in your life.

You'll find more of these praise offerings in Psalms 9, 30, and 118.

Thanksgiving literature isn't prevalent in the Psalms. Yes, there's a lot of material in this book that can be described as thankful in its theme, but true psalms of thanksgiving are rare and include the following—

- an opening statement of praise to God
- a description of the dire circumstances from which God rescued the psalmist
- a description of God's saving actions
- a final statement of praise to God

Packed in between those things are words of wisdom, instruction, testimony, and praise.

The thanksgiving psalms are much more than one person's story of God's saving grace. They're an example to all of us of how intense, genuine, and rich our thanksgiving should be.

▶▶▶Opener (skit option) ▶▶▶▶▶▶▶▶▶▶▶▶▶▶▶▶▶▶

No thanks!

You'll need...
- a copy of **No Thanks!** (page 78), cut apart

Gather students together in the meeting room and divide them into three groups. Give each group one of the situations from the **No Thanks** page. Instruct them to use everyone's input to create an ending for the situation, though not everyone has to be an actor in the skit. After giving them some time to work on this, have each group perform their skit for the entire group. When skits are finished mix students up into groups of four to discuss these questions—

Stepping Back

All of us have things to be thankful for, both big and small, major and minor, visible and invisible. It's time to start telling God thanks on a regular basis.

There's a common misconception about teenagers today. Some people assume that high school students are nothing more than ungrateful so-and-so's. Many of them wear designer clothes, drive their own cars, have spending money, live in nice homes, waste away their free time, and expect everything in life to be handed to them on a platter.

Right.

First of all, everyone who works with teens knows that lumping them into a single general category is a big mistake. For every youth who fits into category A, there are 10 more who don't. That holds true for thankfulness. Some kids have it, some kids know how to

continued next page

- **What did these skits teach you about thankfulness?**
- **What's better—being thankful on the inside without expressing it on the outside or pretending to be thankful on the outside even if you don't feel thankful on the inside? Explain.**
- **Does being thankful change us? How?**
- **Why do you think God wants us to be thankful?**

▶▶▶Opener [artsy/thinking option] ▶▶▶▶▶▶▶▶▶▶▶▶▶▶▶▶

A house of thanks

You'll need...
- paper
- pencils

Give each student a piece of blank paper and a pencil. Begin with something like this—

> **All of us come from different places in life. We've all lived differently, and we've received different types of gifts along the way. Today I'd like you to think about the things that you're thankful for.**

Ask students to tap into their imaginations and envision their lives as large houses. Have them draw a floor plan with different rooms to represent different times in their lives. For example, students might create a living room to portray their early teen years or a nursery to portray their infant years.

After students have had a chance to finish their floor plans, say something like—

> **Now I'd like you to go back through those rooms and think of things that you're thankful for during those times in your life. For example, if you created a room that portrays your infant years, you might include loving parents in that room or good health. Think up several things that you're thankful for in each room and write them in those rooms.**

After a few minutes ask volunteers to share one of the rooms they included in their homes and what they're thankful for in that room. Then ask the following questions—

- **What things in your life have you been the most thankful for?**
- **How does being thankful change you?**
- **How does being thankful change your relationship with God?**

Close either of these openers with something like—

> **Being thankful isn't always our first thought. Today I'd like us to learn more about what it means to be thankful for what God has given us.**

Stepping Back *(cont.)*

express it, and others don't. And of those who don't, some might be ungrateful, yes, but others might have lived lives that have offered them very little to be thankful for. Or maybe they're thankful and just don't know how to express it.

Consider the world that your kids live in. They're bombarded daily with messages telling them that whatever they have isn't enough. They should have more. And when they get more, it should be better than what they already have. You don't see any ads saying, "You don't need anything we have to offer. What you really need is be thankful for what you already have."

Madison Avenue offers our students absolutely nothing in terms of thankfulness.

That's where you need to step in.

Being thankful is relative. Whether you're thankful or not isn't really related to your age, station in life, or financial prosperity. It's more about your heart. Some students in your ministry need a change of heart. They need to know that God gives them countless good things—the least of which isn't salvation and the opportunity to have a relationship with him.

This lesson will help teach your students the value of being thankful.

▶▶▶In the Book ▶▶▶▶▶▶▶▶▶▶▶▶▶▶▶▶▶▶▶▶▶▶▶▶▶

Getting the meat out

You'll need...
- copies of **Getting the Meat Out** (page 79)
- pencils
- Bibles

Introduce this next section with words like these—

> **Have you ever wondered what you should thank God for? Or maybe you know what you want to thank him for, but you don't know how to do it. The psalmist we're going to study today might have had the same difficulty. We're going to see though that he took the time and effort to look at what God had been doing in his life, and then he took the time and effort to thank him for it.**

Divide students into groups of three and give them pencils and copies of **Getting the Meat Out** (page 79). Ask them to read Psalm 118 and write their observations on the handout. When everyone is finished bring the kids back to the center of the meeting room to trade handouts with each other. Reading someone else's observations should help the students discuss the following questions as a large group—

- **What did you learn about thankfulness from reading this psalm?**
- **After reading this psalm how would you define the word *thankful*?**

▶▶▶What it all means (small-group discussion option) ▶▶▶

Thanks, God

You'll need...
- copies of **Thanks, God!** (page 80)
- Bibles

Have students break into groups of four and give each group a copy of **Thanks, God!** (page 80). Allow plenty of time for groups to discuss the questions. When they're finished, call groups to the center of the meeting room and have them share their responses to certain questions of your choice.

Close the small group session by saying something like—

> **Giving God thanks can feel almost impossible at times. We're trying to reach God—and we can't see him. Or we're trying to talk to him—but we keep getting distracted. Whatever the problem is, it's important to make the time to tell God that we're thankful for what he's done in our lives regardless of how we *feel*.**

What it all means (leader-talk option)

The dynamics of gratitude

As you're getting ready to share this talk with your students, have them gather in the center of the meeting room. Give one index card and pencil to each student with instructions to fold the cards in half. The card should now have four useable sides to it. Ask students to write the words *God is working* on one side, *thankfulness* on another side, *reality* on a third side, and *responsibility* on the fourth.

When you're ready begin the talk using the outline below—

God is working

The Psalms remind us that God is at work in our lives. It may feel like he's totally absent until we remember the small stuff. Take a moment to think about the small things that God is doing in your life—giving you good friends, providing you with basic necessities, helping you get along with a brother or sister. Write one thing that God is doing in your life right now under *God is working*.

Give students a few moments to write down what they've thought of. Then continue with—

Be thankful

Once we're reminded what God is doing for us, we've got to thank him. We can thank him privately in prayer, but we can also thank him publicly by telling someone else. Find one other person in the room to share what you're thankful for. Write that person's name on your card under *thankfulness*.

Give students a few moments to share with another person. Then bring them back into one large group and continue with—

Be realistic

You won't always *feel* thankful. Our emotions aren't very reliable things. They change from day to day and moment to moment. Think about something that you *know* you should be thankful for even though you don't *feel* thankful for it. Maybe it's something so ordinary that you take it for granted. Maybe it's something that will be good for you in the long run but you don't really appreciate it now. Write it on your card under *reality*.

Give students a moment to think about something they should be thankful for no matter how they feel. Then conclude with something like this—

Be responsible

God calls us to give thanks for what he's done. Not only does God *give* us stuff, he *commands* that we give him thanks. But that

command isn't like, "You people *must* give me thanks or else!" Instead, he desires that we give him our genuine and heartfelt thanks as our own choice. We're not graded on when or how we give thanks—God leaves that up to us. He just wants us to remember what he's done for us. Think about one way you can express your thanks to God and write it on your card under *responsibility*.

▶▶▶Closing ▶▶▶▶▶▶▶▶▶▶▶▶▶▶▶▶▶▶▶▶▶▶▶▶▶▶▶▶▶

You'll need...
- paper
- pencils

Thanks a million

Ask students to look over the floor plans that they created in the beginning exercise of the lesson. If you didn't create floor plans, begin by having students make a list of five things they're thankful for. Then say something like—

We've seen how one psalmist expressed deep thankfulness for what God has done. Let's take a few minutes to do the same thing.

Have students spread out around the room so they can have privacy. Pass out paper and pencils for them to write their own thankfulness psalms. Guide them through this with the following words, giving them time at the appropriate places—

First I want to write down something about God that you love. Maybe it's his creativity. Maybe it's his faithfulness. Maybe it's his compassion. [Wait]. **Now I want you to write about something that you're thankful for. It can be a specific thing, an event, a person, or anything else you're thankful for.** [Wait]. **Now I want you to write a sentence or two about God's role in the thing you're thankful for. Maybe he created it. Maybe he provided it. Maybe he worked out the circumstances.** [Wait]. **Finally, I want you to write one sentence about *how* you're going to thank God. Maybe you're going to praise him. Maybe you're going to tell another person. Maybe you're going to perform an act of service for someone else.** [Wait]. **What you just did was what the psalmist did—you took time to deliberately express your thanks to God. He loves it when we communicate with him like that.**

Close this session with a prayer like this—

God, we're thankful for so many things in our lives. We're sorry that we don't you thank you for them more often. We want to express our thanks to you all the time because we love you and because we're truly grateful for all you've created and done. Most of all, thank you for loving us enough to send Christ to the world so we could have a relationship with you. We love you. Amen.

NO THANKS!

Read the following situations and determine an appropriate ending.

You're sitting around the Christmas tree and you've just opened the gift you've always wanted—a laptop computer. As you're slitting open the box, your older brother (who got a used car) starts pouting, totally upset that he didn't get a laptop, too.

Read the following situation and determine an appropriate ending.

You've been walking home with your friends for the past seven years. Every day after school, the three of you wander to the corner of the school and wait for the others. One day, one of your friends begins talking about the new bedroom furniture her parents got for her last night.

"Yeah, the bed's real lumpy, and I can't stand the color. My parents just have no idea what I like. They should've talked to me first!"

Last night you watched a TV show that followed the lives of children in a third world country. None of them had floors, let alone bedroom furniture. You're struggling with whether or not you should tell your friend what you saw last night.

Read the following situation and determine an appropriate ending.

You've been sulking around the house all day. Just after lunch you slump into the recliner and begin channel surfing. Your mom walks in and the situation quickly deteriorates.

"Honey, my show's about on. Don't you have some homework to catch up on?"

"Nope."

"Well, look. I paid for that TV, and I work hard for the things I have. This is my time, that's my TV, this is my house, and you need to go find something else to do."

Getting the Meat Out

Read Psalm 118 and write your observations under the appropriate category.

What the psalmist feels	What the psalmist knows	God's actions	Believers' actions	Reasons for thankfulness

THANKS, GOD!

Psalm 118

Before reading this psalm, discuss—
- Was there a time when you felt like God blessed you with something unbelievable? Explain.
- What's the purpose of giving thanks to God?
- What happens if you refuse to give God thanks?

Read Psalm 18.

Verses 1-7
- Why does the psalmist say we should thank God?
- Describe the relationship between the psalmist and God.
- When have you been set free from something?
- What was your response to God?

Verses 8-9
- What do you think the psalmist means in these two verses?

Verses 10-16
- How did the psalmist *cut off* his enemies?
- How do you think the name of the Lord saves us?
- How does the psalmist describe God in verse 14? What do you think he means?
- Do we have to be free from sin before God will rescue us?
- Who are the *righteous* described in verse 15?

Verses 17-21
- What is the psalmist's response to God in verses 17, 19, and 21?
- How does God *become our salvation*?
- The psalmist gives thanks because God answered him. Has God ever answered you? When and how?
- Should we be thankful even if God isn't answering us?

Verses 22-29
- What does the psalmist think of God? How does he express that?
- What do you think of God? How do you express that?

After you've read this psalm, discuss—
- How do you think God defines thankfulness?
- What did you learn from this psalm about thankfulness?

How to hear God **Psalm 95**

Oracle Psalms

Oracle. *Revelation, divine communication, truth, advice, judgment, answer, prophecy.* That's what an oracle psalm contains. Somewhere in the middle of the psalmist's words, God speaks. And when he speaks, he wants and expects us to listen.

The psalms as a whole really are tools to teach us how to communicate with God. "The Psalms come from a people who hear God speak to them and realize that it is the most important word they will ever hear spoken. They decide to respond. They answer" (E. Peterson, *Answering God*, p. 14).

Of course we can't respond to God if we don't first hear him. And we can't hear him if we aren't listening. And we can't listen if we're busy or surrounded by noise. So how do we learn to listen to God? When does he speak? How do we begin recognizing his voice?

In Psalm 95, God speaks in the middle of a worship service. This psalm was intended to by recited by a priest to the assembled Israelites. According to one commentator, official representatives of God—pastors or priests, for example—sometimes shifted to first person when speaking for him (*NIV Study Bible*, note on Psalm 95:9]. God spoke through humans. In this particular psalm, it's almost as if God were standing there, listening to his congregation sing a hymn, and at just the right moment, when he's sure to get their attention, he breaks in with a warning. "Don't forget what happened in the past."

For some other examples, look up Psalms 75 and 82.

But God speaks to us in other ways, too. The beginning of this psalm talks about the majesty of creation. Certainly when we take the time to examine what God has made, we can hear him speak to us. And how about during worship—when we are gathered with fellow believers, singing to God as a unified body. Isn't it likely that God will speak to us through the actions of those around us?

God *spoke* the universe into existence. The gospel of John calls Jesus the *Word*. Certainly language is one of the most profound gifts of communication God provided for us. It makes sense, then, doesn't it, that God continues to speak to us today?

Stepping Back

God spoke. God speaks. God is speaking.

Yada yada.

Most of us don't doubt that God speaks. The problem is—how do we hear him?

Your students get spoken at nonstop. The TV speaks at them. Their parents speak at them. Their teachers speak at them. *You* probably speak at them. At some point, they've all learned how to tune out the things they don't want to hear so they can enjoy a few moments of quiet.

Walking around telling your kids that God speaks to them today might raise some eyebrows. First of all, they might not want one more person speaking at them. And secondly, they might think that all he speaks about is sin and judgment and stuffy theological issues. Who wants to listen to all that nonsense?

Your job is to let your kids know not only that God speaks but that what

continued next page

You'll need...

- a sound effects CD or prerecorded tape of 10 familiar sounds
- a CD or tape player
- paper
- pencils

▶▶▶Opener (listening option)▶▶▶▶▶▶▶▶▶▶▶▶▶▶▶▶▶

Name that sound

Before the meeting, get a sound effects CD or record some common sounds like a telephone ringing, someone talking, a second of a popular song, and so on. You'll also need to write down or remember the sounds you've recorded since you'll be asking students to name them.

When everyone has arrived begin with something like this—

Today you're getting tested. I'm going to play a CD for you, but you'll have to listen closely. Let's see how well you can do.

Stepping Back *(cont.)*

he has to say is meaningful for their lives. Once they begin to hear his voice, they won't need any more convincing from you.

Hand out paper and pencils and instruct students *not* to write anything until you tell them. Play the CD or tape for students softly so they have to pay attention. When you're finished tell them to write down all the sounds they heard that they can remember. Play the CD or tape again, this time letting students write as they're listening. When everyone is finished, check their answers. Then ask these questions—

Sometimes it's hard to identify a sound if it's quiet or if it's not in its normal context. Paying closer attention can help. Focusing can help. Probably the most helpful thing, though, is to be very quiet and still so the sound is clear.

You'll need...

- copies of **Difficult Directions** (page 86) cut in squares

▶▶▶Opener (group-activity option)▶▶▶▶▶▶▶▶▶▶▶▶▶▶▶

Whadidya say?

Gather students in the center of the meeting room and give each youth one square from the handout. Tell them that on your signal, they are to do exactly what's on their paper. Let chaos reign for several minutes and then sit them down to discuss these questions—

- **What did you just experience?**
- **Were you able to pay attention to what other people were doing?**
- **What's difficult about listening to people in this environment?**

Close either of these openers by saying something like—

Listening to God is a lot like what you just experienced here. There are lots of things that compete with God's voice in our lives. Today we're going to look at a psalm that encourages us to pay close attention to what God has to say to us.

▶▶▶In the Book ▶▶▶▶▶▶▶▶▶▶▶▶▶▶▶▶▶▶▶▶▶▶

Historic listeners

Assemble your kids into groups of four to six and say something like—

> **People have struggled with listening to God for centuries. And they've not just struggled with being able to hear God; they've also had to deal with what God was telling them. I'd like you to look at the lives of some old-timers who heard from God.**

You'll need...
- copies of **People Who Listened** (page 87)
- pencils
- Bibles

Distribute pencils and copies of **People Who Listened** (page 87) to each group. When they're finished have groups share what they learned. Then ask—

- **What did you learn about how God sometimes speaks to people?**
- **What did you learn about what God has said to people in the past?**
- **Do you think God always has bad news for people? Explain.**

> **God still speaks to people today, but in different ways. The main way God speaks to us now is through the Bible—his Word—which is filled with his advice, training, encouragement, and comfort.**

▶▶▶What it all means (self-assessment option) ▶▶▶▶▶▶▶▶

What I'm listening to

You'll need...
- copies of **What I'm Listening To** (page 88)
- pencils

Hand each student a pencil and a copy of **What I'm Listening To** (page 88) and begin like this—

> **Listening to God isn't always easy, especially with everything that competes for our attention. I'd like you to consider for a moment what things keep you from hearing God's voice.**

Ask students to think about the things that compete for their attention and categorize them under one of the three headings—Sin, Busyness, or Focus. Pair students up to share their responses. Then invite volunteers to share with the entire class. Encourage further discussion with some questions—

- **What did you learn about yourself through identifying these things?**
- **What did you learn about listening to God?**
- **What thing did you hear that you weren't expecting?**

Conclude with something like—

We've got to clear some things out of our lives before we can hear God's voice. And hearing God is important—important enough to give up some of the hindrances.

You'll need...

- copies of **What's That You Say, God?** (page 89)
- pencils
- Bibles

▶▶▶What it all means (discussion option)▶▶▶▶▶▶▶▶▶▶

What's that you say, God?

Distribute pencils and copies of **What's That You Say, God?** (page 89) to students grouped in fours. Allow plenty of time for discussion and then bring everyone together to share some of their answers.

Close the small group session by saying something like—

The writer of this psalm was seeking to praise God. In the middle of his praise, God spoke. It would have been easy to miss God's voice. If the psalmist had been so caught up in his own agenda—praise—he might never have heard God. It takes deliberate effort on our part to always keep our ears open for God's voice.

You'll need...

- a candle
- matches

▶▶▶What it all means (leader-talk option)▶▶▶▶▶▶▶▶▶▶

The sounds of silence

Okay, we're agreed that listening to God is important. But how do we help our students with that? For this lesson you're going to skip talking at your students. Instead you're going to give them something they rarely have—10 minutes of total silence. Tell them to view this time as a gift from you—a gift of time away from TV, music, parents, friends, and all the other noise of the world.

If you feel you need to, it's okay to play soft, instrumental music while students are experiencing this. However, don't crank the music too loud—that might prevent students from getting all that they can from this exercise.

Begin by dimming the lights. Then place a lighted candle in the center of your meeting room. Instruct your students to find a place where they can be comfortable. Ask them to slowly let go of all that's happened during the day. Suggest that they picture themselves walking or sitting with Jesus. Then say something like—

The first step to hearing God is being silent and listening. I'm going to give you 10 minutes of total silence to listen for God's voice. You might want to begin by asking God to speak to you. It could be through images, words, or thoughts. God promises that if we seek him, we will find him. You might not hear God so much

as sense him or see him. That's fine. This time is yours to be alone with God.

This could be a very strange experience for your students. They're not used to silence. They're not used to focusing intently on something invisible. Your actions will set the tone for this activity. If it's possible and if you have the leaders available to help, you may want to consider letting kids spread out into other places in addition to your meeting room.

When the 10 minutes are up, don't ask students to share about their experience in front of the group. Instead, invite them to contact you in the next few days to tell you what they learned.

Closing

Hearing prayers

Have students get in pairs. Say something like—

You've seen that God wants to speak to us. And you've discovered what things might prevent us from hearing his voice. Today I'd like you to make a renewed commitment to listen to God.

Ask pairs to share one thing that they'd like to hear God's voice about in their lives. Students might say they want to know God's will or want guidance about where they should go to college. When they're finished sharing have students pray for each other. Then close the session with words like these—

God, we know that you speak to your children. Sometimes, though, we have a hard time hearing you. Help us get rid of the distractions that take our focus off you. Help us learn how to listen to your voice. Help us to hear your words to us when we read the Bible. We want to hear your voice. Amen.

Difficult Directions

Walk around giving advice about how to study the Bible.

Walk around talking loudly about the last test you took in school.

Walk around telling people about the best date you can imagine.

Walk around asking people how their last birthday went.

Walk around giving people high fives and telling them to have a great game.

Walk around helping people with whatever they've been assigned to do in this activity.

Walk around asking people for directions to the bathroom.

Walk around arranging people in groups of four and asking them to recite the Pledge of Allegiance.

People Who Listened

What I'm listening to

Write down things that compete for your attention. Categorize them under one of the three headings—sin, busyness, or focus.

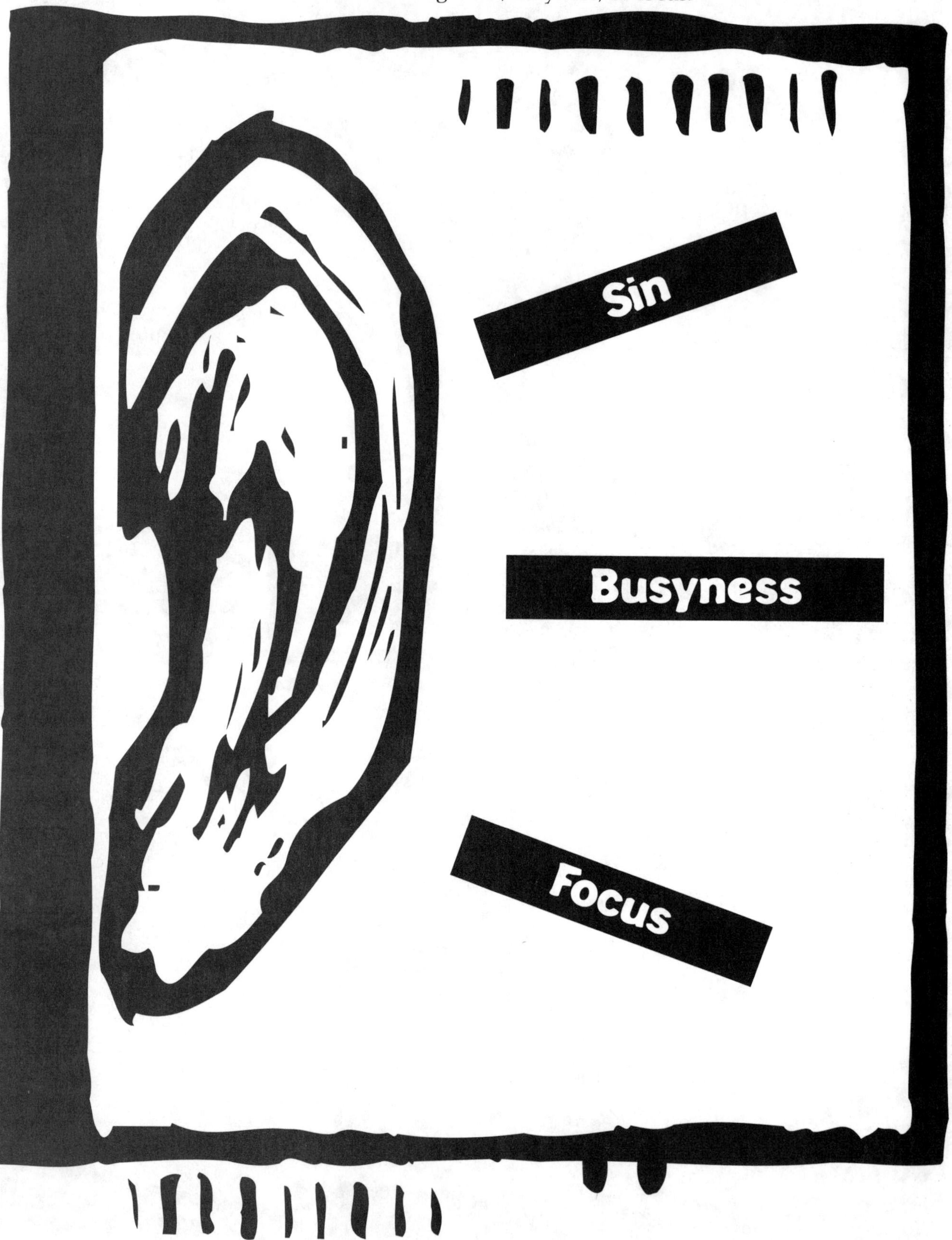

WHAT'S THAT YOU SAY, GOD? Psalm 95

Before reading this passage, discuss—
- When have you heard God's voice?
- What types of things does God tell people?
- Should people who say God speaks to them be suspect? Why?

Read Psalm 95.

Verses 1-2
- What does this passage say about worshiping God?
- Is there a right or a wrong way to worship God?
- What are some essential for worship?

Verses 3-5
- How does God's creation speak to us?
- If God is so great, why doesn't he speak audibly, so we can hear him?

Verses 6-11
- How does God speak to us in worship?
- What other ways does God speak to us?
- How does our attitude hinder us from hearing God?
- What are the results of listening to God?
- What are the benefits of listening to God?
- What are the results of ignoring God?

After reading the psalm, discuss—
- What do you think God's voice sounds like?
- Talk about a time when you know you heard God's voice. What did God say to you?
- Does everyone hear God's voice in the same way? Explain.

Battle lines are drawn **Psalm 52**

Taunt Psalms

The taunt psalms—they're the ones that make us squirm in discomfort when we read them. So much hatred. So much animosity. So much vengeance. Taunt psalms seem to go against everything Christ taught about loving our enemies, turning the other cheek, and being a good neighbor to everyone.

It's important to understand where the taunt psalms came from. During the Old Testament era when God was establishing Israel as his covenant people, there were countless other nations trying to destroy her. And in the process, those nations were trying to destroy God's rule on earth. They were pagan peoples who didn't believe in God and most certainly didn't accept his claim to be the one and only deity.

The enemies spoken of in taunt psalms weren't just the meanies who lived across the street and made life miserable for the psalmist. They were the people who denied and defied God. They were the people who, in the words of Psalm 52, *love evil rather than good, falsehood rather than speaking the truth.* They were not personal enemies out to get an individual so much as they were spiritual enemies out to get God's chosen people.

Eugene Peterson says, "Prayer is combat. Prayer brings us before God—and there, before God, we find ourselves grappling with the world rulers of this present darkness, against the spiritual hosts of wickedness in the heavenly places (Ephesians 6:12)" (*Answering God,* p. 95).

These are the enemies the psalmists talked to God about. "It is an act of profound faith to entrust one's most precious hatreds to God, knowing they will be taken seriously" (Walter Brueggermann, *The Message of the Psalms*, p. 77). Hatred is not God's will for our lives. But it does serve a purpose. "Our hate is used by God to bring the enemies of life and salvation to notice...while hate provides the necessary spark for ignition, it is the wrong fuel for the engines of judgment; only love is adequate to sustain these passions" (Peterson, p. 102).

Knowing this should keep us from squirming when we read the taunt psalms. It should help us see that the message of the Old Testament is

Intrigued? Read on. You can find other examples in Psalms 53, 115, and 135.

Stepping Back

We've all felt hatred toward someone or something. The only thing deserving of our hatred is evil—the real enemy. And the best thing we can do with that hatred is give it to God.

This probably seems like a pretty heavy topic for your students. Hatred, evil, enemies, the powers of darkness. Where did all the sweet little psalms go?

But here's the reality of the world—your students are bombarded with the enemy's false messages everyday. *Your worth is based on your appearance. Material possessions are where it's at. Success is measured in dollars. You deserve whatever you want. You're just some cosmic accident that has no purpose. God is whatever or whoever you want him to be.*

Those are messages that deserve to be hated. Think of all the misguided people. Think of all the lies being swallowed by

continued next page

not opposite of the message of the New Testament. Evil is deserving of our hatred. But that hatred should be given to God where he can transform it into his purpose for our lives, and where ultimately, he can teach us to love our enemies.

Stepping Back *(cont.)*

young people. *That's* something worth fighting against.

Ultimately, however, the battle is not ours but the Lord's—a phrase right out of the Psalms. We can't win anything on our own. But neither can we help God in this struggle if we never take the time to identify and recognize the real enemy.

Your students need to know that their real enemy is not the kid at school who annoys them or the teacher who's always on their case—though they may *feel* like real enemies. The real enemies are those who promote the lies of the devil...that God doesn't exist, that life has no meaning, that there is no purpose for anyone's existence. Once your students realize this, they will be in a position to fight on God's side of the battlelines.

Opener (discussion option)

A message to my enemies

Introduce the exercise like this—

> **We've all known someone who really bothered us. Someone who, for whatever reason, succeeded in ruining our lives for a small amount of time. Listen to this story about that kind of situation.**

Read "**Lies and Twisted Truth**" on **Imperfect Enemies** (page **97**). When you're finished reading, say something like—

> **Imagine that this happened to you. You've got a chance to tell Heather how you feel because the principal is calling the two of you into her office. She's going to give each of you time to air your problems. What would you say?**

Assemble your students in groups of four. Give groups time to discuss what they'd say to Heather, then have them share their thoughts with the rest of the class. Then say something like—

> **If this really happened to you, it would be easy to view Heather as your enemy. She was mean. She lied. She got you in trouble. There's nothing about her that you like. Though the psalms often identified and got angry with enemies, the Bible still tells us to love everyone.**

- **Is it okay to treat someone badly when they've treated you badly first?**
- **If someone does what Heather did, what would be your likely reaction?**
- **When have you been the object of someone's attacks? What did you do?**
- **How can we love people we're mad at?**

▶▶▶Opener (drama option) ▶▶▶▶▶▶▶▶▶▶▶▶▶▶▶▶▶▶▶▶

Imperfect enemies

You'll need...
- copies of **Imperfect Enemies** (page 97)

Have students pair up, then open with this question—

Have you ever known someone who had an unfounded desire to destroy or hurt you? I'd like us to talk about that today.

Give each pair a copy of **Imperfect Enemies**. Assign a quarter of the pairs to create an *imperfect* responses to the *first* scenario, a quarter to create a *perfect* response to the *first* scenario, a quarter to create an *imperfect* response to the *second* scenario, and a quarter to create a perfect response to the *second* scenario. Have them read their situation and develop a sketch of what they'd say and do if they were under attack like their scenario presents. When the pairs have had a few minutes to prepare, have them share their sketches. Then ask these questions and others you may think of after you see the performances.

- **When have you treated an enemy poorly?**
- **Is it more spiritual to treat enemies nicely than poorly?**
- **When have you been the object of someone's attacks? What did you do?**

Close either of these openers by saying something like—

Everyone has had an enemy now and then. It can be really difficult dealing with people who seem interested in hurting us for no apparent reason. Today we're going to look at a psalm that will help us learn how to deal with our enemies.

▶▶▶What it all means (advice-giving option) ▶▶▶▶▶▶▶▶▶▶▶

Enemies in my life

You'll need...
- copies of **Imperfect Enemies** (page 97)
- pencils
- paper
- Bibles

Open this section with something like—

We've seen how the psalmist felt about his enemy. Now let's see what Jesus said about how we should act toward those who hate us.

Ask students to get in pairs and read Matthew 5:43-48. Have them rewrite the verse using their own words. When pairs have shared their new verses with the class, ask them—

- **What does it mean to love our enemies? Explain.**

- **Do you think loving our enemies has to do with our feelings or our actions? Explain.**
- **Do Jesus' words from Matthew contradict the message of this psalm? Explain.**

Continue the lesson something like this—

> **It can be difficult to actually put these principles into practice. Let's see if we can come up with some practical ways to love our enemies.**

Give groups copies of **Imperfect Enemies** that you might have used in the opener. Ask the kids to reread Matthew 5:43-48 and think about how they might apply the love-your-enemies theme to these situations. Give groups time to write out some advice to the person in each situation. When they're finished, have groups share the advice they offered.

You'll need...
- copies of **When Enemies Attack** (page 98)
- Bibles

▸▸▸What it all means (discussion option)▸▸▸▸▸▸▸▸▸▸▸

When enemies attack

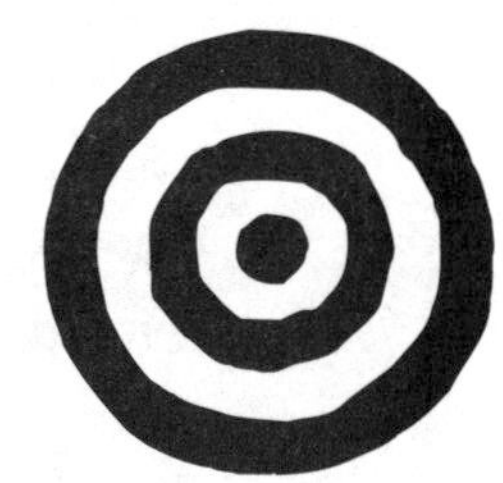

Gather youths into groups of four and pass out copies of **When Enemies Attack** (page 98). Have groups discuss the questions on the sheet and share their responses with everyone.

Close the small group session by saying something like—

> **We've all had to deal with an enemy at some point in our lives. This psalm outlines the real emotions of someone dealing with an enemy. Did you notice how the psalmist ultimately found his refuge in God? Whatever our experience with enemies, God helps us.**

You'll need...
- whiteboard
- markers

▸▸▸What it all means (leader-talk option)▸▸▸▸▸▸▸▸▸▸▸

The *real* enemy

Use the following ideas to formulate your talk—

> **When you read the psalms, it might seem as though people in the Old Testament were meaner, more vengeful, and more violent than those in the New Testament. They talk about hating their enemies. They ask God to defeat their enemies. Their deepest desire to see their enemies destroyed. It doesn't sound like there's much love, does it? But it's important to understand that, even though God never changes, people and society do. In the Old Testament, when people spoke of enemies, they were almost always talking about people who were opposed to God and his chosen people—the Jews.**

On the whiteboard make a list of things that describe the enemy in Psalm 52. Ask kids to help you. Some of these should be—deceitful, loves evil rather than good, lies, doesn't make God his stronghold, trusts in money rather than God, destroys others in pursuit of power.

Continue with something like—

The psalmist said some strong things about his enemy. He called him "a disgrace in God's eyes." He said, "Surely God will bring you down to everlasting ruin." It sure sounds like the psalmist hated his enemy. But he didn't *act* on his hate. Instead, he talked to God about it. Doing this helped clarify the issues for him. The psalmist had a legitimate gripe. This person was totally opposed to God and truth. *That* is who our real enemy is.

Have students come up with a list of the things our real enemies believe. Rather than identifying individual enemies, have them identify the enemy's message. For example—*a person's beauty determines their value. Success is based on how much money a person makes. Material possessions are the source of true happiness. God is everywhere, in everyone, in whatever form you imagine him to be. Having sex before marriage with someone you really love is okay.*

Then continue with—

When it comes right down to it, our real enemy usually isn't a certain person, even if it feels like it now and then. Our enemy is evil. Remember in the Lord's Prayer when Jesus said, "Deliver us from evil"? That should be our prayer, too. Evil is anything that goes against the truth of God. Jesus called Satan the father of lies—he is the source of evil. When we're feeling hatred toward someone, we should tell God, just like the psalmist did. Then we should take a minute to think about this—our hatred is better directed toward the evil in the world than it is toward a person we don't much care for. Jesus commanded us to love our enemies—the people who persecute us. But he didn't command us to love evil. Jesus is the perfect model for us of someone who loved those who hated him, but who hated the evil things that filled the world.

Closing

Responsive reading

We've seen a lot today about dealing with an enemy. To wrap things up, I'd like you to consider how you'll treat an enemy of yours. I'm going to ask us to enter into a traditional worship form—responsive reading. After I read a sentence, you reply with the statement, "Help us love our enemies."

Dear God, sometimes we feel persecuted by people who hate us.
Help us love our enemies.

There are even times when we feel like you've forgotten us and left us to weather the attacks by ourselves.
Help us love our enemies.

It can feel impossible to love people when they attack us, God.
Help us love our enemies.

We need to have your heart and your spirit help us when it's impossible to love the people who are trying to hurt us.
Help us love our enemies.

When these enemies attack, we need to know you're there for us.
Help us love our enemies.

When we feel alone, we need to know that you're comforting us.
Help us love our enemies.

God, please deliver us from evil.
Help us love our enemies.

Imperfect Enemies

Read the following situations and think about how you would respond to the attacks.

Lies and Twisted Truth

You and Heather have never been friends. You never hang out and you never go to the same parties. You don't really know her.

Yesterday, Gail told you that Heather has been saying all kinds of really horrible things about you. Seems she's been telling people you're a heavy drinker—though you don't drink at all—and that you're a liar. All morning today your friends don't seem to want to talk to you. Some have even been ignoring you.

You see Heather passing you in the hall, so you decide to ask her what's up. "Heather, why are you saying all these things about me?"

"Look, I don't want to talk to you. You're pure evil, and I hate you!" She's talking really loud, and it appears that she's looking around to see who's listening.

"Heather, I don't know what you're doing. Why won't you just stop this?"

Suddenly, Heather ducks, like you've just taken a swing at her, then she stands up and socks you in the face. Things get hazy. Just before you lose consciousness, you hear, "Did you see that? She took a swing at me!"

The next thing you know, you're waking up on the floor. The nurse and the principal are standing over you. The principal is talking to your dad on her cell phone. "Mr. Keating, I'd like you to come get your daughter. I'm suspending her for a week for fighting."

As you walk away you see Heather standing with your friends. They're consoling her and giving you dirty looks.

Sticks on the Roof

You walk home from school the same way every day. Today you had this really awful experience.

As you passed Mr. Colter's house, he was outside looking at his roof. You've known these neighbors all your life. Mr. Colter sees you coming and he begins to wave his cane at you and yell. At first, you want to go talk to him. But he looks upset and angry, so you decide to stay at the gate.

"Young man!" he begins, "Do you see those sticks on my roof? Did you throw them there? I'm positive you did. I'm going to tell your parents about it. I'll get you good for messing up my roof."

You can't believe it. You head home and the minute you walk into the house your mom is after you. "Honey, why did you throw those sticks on Mr. Colter's roof? He's been over here three times today to complain about it."

Three weeks have passed now. Mr. Colter has called you and your parents every day to talk about those sticks. You even went over to clean off his roof, but that didn't stop him. He's even begun standing outside his house in the mornings to tell you what a rotten person you are for what you did.

The truth is, you have absolutely no idea how those sticks got there.

When Enemies Attack Psalm 52

Before you read this psalm—

- Talk about a time when you felt like the target of injustice.
- Talk about a time when you were being attacked and wanted to fight back, but didn't.
- Answer the question: When I feel attacked I should _______________ .

Read Psalm 52.

Verses 1-4

- What destructive qualities does the "mighty man" have?
- If you could draw a picture of the type of person who loves hurting others, what would you include?
- What's the result of boasting in evil? What's the difference between someone who does this and someone who doesn't?

Verses 5-7

- Is it right to wish God's judgment on *people* who are evil? Explain.
- How can we hate *evil* but still love our *enemies*?

Verses 8-9

- Why do you think the psalmist includes this description of a righteous person?
- What are some of the differences between this person and the person in verses 1-4?

After you've read the psalm, discuss—

- Does the beginning of this passage describe anyone or anything you know?
- How do you deal with that person or thing right now?
- Will you do anything differently after studying this psalm?

There is comfort even for the abandoned **Psalm 31**

Complaint Psalms

Here's some more to check out—Psalms 13, 17, 54, 55, and 70.

Yeah, we talked about these already. For background info, check back with session four. For more specifics about this lesson, forge ahead.

Stepping Back

All of us have felt alone, abandoned, and forgotten. The psalmist shows us that when we feel that way, we can tell God all about it knowing that he'll listen.

So why do the complaint psalms get double duty in this book? If you take the time to read through the entire book of Psalms, you'll notice that a good number of the poems are complaints. Why is that? In his book on the Psalms and prayer, Eugene Peterson says, "Prayer is the language of the people who are in trouble and know it, and who believe or hope that God can get them out." (*Answering God*, p. 36.) He then goes on to quote Isaac Bashevis Singer who once said, "I only pray when I am in trouble. But I am in trouble all the time, and so I pray all the time."

Ah-ha.

It's the truth, isn't it? More often than not, we are in trouble. It's part of

continued next page

▶▶▶Opener (large-group option) ▶▶▶▶▶▶▶▶▶▶▶▶▶

Nonmusical chairs

Before students arrive set up the chairs in your room in the following way:

- Set three chairs together in a circle.
- Set a group of five chairs in a line side by side.
- Set several single chairs throughout the room, where no other chairs are near.
- Set several chairs together in the center of the room.

Tell students as they arrive that they can sit anywhere in the room they want, but they can't move any of the chairs. When students have found a place to sit, say something like—

> **When you came in tonight, how did you decide where to sit? Did you want to be with other people? Alone? Did you wait to see where your friends sat first so you could join them, or did you trust that they'd join you wherever you were sitting? Feeling left out is never pleasant.**

Ask students to look around them and then ask these questions—

- **What does this room demonstrate about abandonment?**
- **What does this room demonstrate about people who are left out of a group?**

Stepping Back *(cont.)*

being human. Because Christ himself was fully human, he understands the trouble we are in. And so what do we do? We tell him about it. We lay open our hearts, bare our emotions, and say, "Help me!"

In lesson four, we looked at a complaint psalm that deals with all the emotions surrounding a person who feels attacked and persecuted. This time we'll look at a complaint psalm that deals with all the emotions surrounding a person who feels alone and abandoned. All our students have been there.

Today's teens live in a subculture all their own. They have their own music, their own television shows, their own radio stations, their own fashions, their own schools, their own church programs...we have successfully managed to push them into their own space. We don't want them in our

continued next page

- **What should we do for people who feel left out of a group?**
- **How does God feel about people who are left out or abandoned?**

Opener (picture-evaluation option)

You are here

You'll need...
- copies of **Where Are You?** (page 104)
- pencils

As students arrive ask them to find a place in the room where they can have a bit of privacy. Give each of them a copy of **Where Are You?** (page 104) and a pencil. Begin this opener by saying something like—

> **Today we're going to talk about feeling lonely and abandoned. I want you to look at this picture and think about where you might fit in it. If you see someone that you identify with, write your name above that person. If you don't find yourself in the picture, draw yourself in and write what you're doing there.**

Give students a few minutes to work with their pictures. When they're finished have them pair up to share their responses. Gather everyone in a circle and ask the following questions—

- **How do you think each person (or group of people) in the picture feels?**
- **What does this picture communicate about feeling left out or abandoned?**
- **Describe a time you've felt left out or abandoned.**

Close either of these openers by saying something like—

> **All of us have felt left out or abandoned at one time or another. It may feel hard to believe that anyone else can really understand what it feels like. Today we're going to look at a psalm written by a person who understood exactly how it felt to be left out, lonely, and abandoned by other people.**

In the Book

Emotional outpourings

You'll need...
- whiteboard and markers
- Bibles

Begin the activity like this—

> **We're going to look at a passage of Scripture that reveals an emotion we all sometimes feel. As we look at this psalm, we'll learn a bit about how we can handle ourselves when we feel like everyone has abandoned us.**

The psalmist here was obviously distressed. He expressed his feelings with some very descriptive lines like "My eyes grow weak with sorrow" and "I have become like broken pottery." Take a few minutes to read this psalm silently.

If some of your students don't have Bibles, be sure to have extras available. After giving them time to read the psalm, continue with—

Look at verses 9-13. Let's make a list of all the phrases the psalmist uses to describe his feelings.

Let students call out their answers while you or someone else writes them on the board. Then go on with—

Now look at verses 14-24. Here the psalmist talks about what he's going to do with all his feelings of distress. Let's list those, too.

Again, let students call out their answers to be written on the board. Some are very obvious, like "I trust in you," while others are more subtle, like "Be strong and take heart." You may need to help kids read between the lines for some of those. When they're finished, continue with—

Why did the psalmist react that way? Why didn't he just give up and let his distress overtake him? Because he knew and believed certain things about God. Look at verses 19-24 to see what those things were.

Once again, list your students' answers on the board. Then move on to the next section.

Stepping Back *(cont.)*

way, but we do want them where we can keep an eye on them. (For more insight into this phenomenon, read *A Tribe Apart* by Patricia Hersch).

So what's the worst thing that could happen to a teen? Being rejected or abandoned by their own. Not fitting in. Being outside the inner circle. Not belonging to any certain group.

Being alone.

This psalm has a lot to say to your students about how they can turn to God when they're feeling like that.

▶▶▶What it all means (small-group creative option) ▶▶▶▶▶

Abandoned situations

You'll need...

- copies of **Feeling Abandoned** (page 105)
- pencils
- paper

Move into the next section by saying something like—

We've seen what the psalmist did when he felt abandoned, but what about us? Is there anything we can do for ourselves or other people when it seems like there's no one who cares?

Give each group of four students a copy of **Friendly Abandonment** (page 105). Assign one situation to each group. Based on what they learned from the first activity, have them offer advice to the person with the problem, perhaps in a Dear Abby-style letter. Have each group tell its advice or read its letter to the rest of the class. Then ask—

What should we do when we see that our friends feel abandoned?
- **Do you think people who are feeling abandoned or lonely want**

If you need a song to set the tone or create an emotion at any part of this study, consider using Jennifer Knapp's song "Hold Me Now" from her *Kansas* album.

advice? Explain.

- **Do you agree or disagree with this statement: *God never abandons us.* Explain.**
- **When you've felt abandoned, what helped you get through it?**

What it all means (small-group discussion option)

Understanding abandonment

You'll need...
- copies of **Understanding Abandonment** (page 106)
- Bibles

Have students gather in groups of four. Give each group a copy of **Understanding Abandonment** (page 106), and have them discuss the questions on the sheet. When they're finished have groups share some of their responses.

Close the small group session by saying something like—

> **Feeling abandoned isn't pleasant. However, this psalm helps us see that it's a natural human emotion. This psalm also points out that there is one person who always listens to us when we're feeling that way...God.**

What it all means (leader-talk option)

You'll need...
- file labels or mailing labels
- markers

It's okay to complain to God

Hand out a marker and several labels to each student. Use the following as an outline for your talk—

> **It's okay to *feel* abandoned.**
>
> **All of us at some point have felt like no one cares about us. Maybe we've even felt like God has forgotten about us. If you haven't felt like this yet, there will be a day. There are many different reasons why we feel abandoned. I want you to think of some and write each on a separate label.**

When kids have finished writing, continue with—

> **It's okay to feel upset.**
>
> **Sometimes when we feel upset about something, we start to feel guilty. For some reason we thing it's wrong to be mad about our circumstances or to feel sad because we're lonely. But it's not wrong. God created our emotions. The problem isn't how we're *feeling*. The problem is letting our feelings get the best of us.**
>
> **It's okay to complain to God.**
>
> **Sometimes just telling someone else how we're feeling does a**

lot for us. That's why telling God about what's going on is so important. God can handle your anger, your sadness, your loneliness, and your worst feelings of abandonment. In fact, he's the *only* one who can handle them. Remember, he knows you inside and out anyway.

▶▶▶Closing ▶▶▶▶▶▶▶▶▶▶▶▶▶▶▶▶▶▶▶▶▶▶▶▶▶▶▶

I feel alone

You'll need...
- paper
- pencils
- labels from the leader talk (optional)

Ask students to find a place in the room where they can have some privacy, then say something like—

We've talked a lot today about feeling abandoned, left out, and even forgotten by everyone. I'd like you to write a letter to God about a time when you've felt abandoned.

Distribute paper and pencils. Instruct students to take the labels they filled out during the leader talk option and put them on their paper as a reminder of what makes them feel abandoned. If you didn't give the leader talk (and, therefore, don't have the labels), spend a few minutes brainstorming reasons why they might feel abandoned. Then give students several minutes to write their letters. When they're finished close with a prayer like this—

God, it's hard to feel abandoned. We all want to belong, to fit in, to be part of the crowd. When we feel left out, it hurts deeply. We know that you understand how it feels to be abandoned by your friends. Truthfully, we wish we never had to feel that way. But when we do, help us to remember that you're always there, that you care about our hurts, that you know when we feel alone and abandoned. Help us hang on to you tightly through those times. Amen.

where are you?

Can you identify with someone in this picture? If so, who? If not, draw yourself in.

FEELING ABANDONED

Read through the following situations and offer some advice on how to handle them.

SHELBY

Shelby and Rayanne have been best friends for years. They've been cheerleading together since they started high school three years ago.

Last week Rayanne began avoiding Shelby and started hanging out with Erin, a new girl in school. Today Shelby asked Rayanne if she wanted to come over to study. Rayanne said she couldn't and added that her schedule's getting really busy and she probably wouldn't be able to do anything with her for a while. Shelby knows it's because she's spending all her time with Erin.

ZACH

Zach has been feeling left out at home lately. It seems like his parents are always gushing over the things his younger brothers do. They never do that for him. In fact, it seems like they're always disappointed in him, whether it's how he's doing at school or the way he dresses or the friends he hangs with. Last night, when he got home from work, the house was empty. They'd all gone out for dinner and a movie. All he got was a note saying, "Out for a while. Back at 9:30. Be sure to finish your homework and pick up your room."

BRANDON

Brandon's dad hasn't been himself lately. It's easy to understand because he was laid off three months ago and his job search hasn't been that successful. Adding to the pressure, Ben's mom got a great paying job across town.

His dad stays at home all day—alone. When Ben gets home from school, his dad is still in his underwear. Yesterday, Ben asked his dad how things were going, and his dad just yelled at him. Ben's mom says that his dad feels like no one cares about him.

Understanding Abandonment

Psalm 31

Before you read this psalm—

- Describe a time when you felt abandoned or left out
- What should you do when you feel like that
- What does it mean to be abandoned?

Read Psalm 31.

Verses 1-8

- When have you felt like the writer of this psalm felt
- Who else do you know who feels like this?
- Why does God allow us to feel like this?
- What should we do when we feel like this?

Verses 9-13

- Describe a time you've felt abandoned by your friends.
- When you felt that way, did it seem like God had left you, too? Explain.
- Do you think everyone feels abandoned at some time?

Verses 14-24

- How does the psalmist deal with his feelings of abandonment?
- How do you deal with your feelings of abandonment?
- Does telling God about your bad feelings make then go away? Explain.
- Does the security that God offers help when you feel abandoned?

After reading this psalm, discuss—

- What does this passage say about being abandoned?
- What doesn't this passage say about being abandoned?
- What should you do when you've *been* abandoned?

Why we take time out of the journey in order to worship
Psalm 122

Songs of Ascents

When you look at the book of Psalms as a whole, it's a mish-mash. A complaint psalm here, a taunt psalm there, a torah psalm here, a blessing psalm there. But tucked in near the end, all together in a complete unit, is a type of book within a book—the Songs of Ascents.

These 15 psalms—Psalms 120-134—were sung by the Hebrew pilgrims as they journeyed to Jerusalem to worship several times a year. Because Jerusalem had the highest elevation of any city in Palestine, the Hebrews literally ascended to get to its borders. But any Christian with even a smidgeon of imagination can grasp the deeper meaning of *ascend*. Life for a Christian is a daily journey deeper into God—maturity—and upward toward God—holiness. C. S. Lewis captured this idea in his final episode of the Chronicles of Narnia, *The Last Battle*, when Aslan tells his followers to travel "further up and further in." The Apostle Paul captured the same idea in Philippians 3:14 when he said, "I *press on toward* the goal to win the prize for which God has called me *heavenward* in Christ Jesus."

This journey we are on as Christ-followers does not consist of merely coasting. It consists of deliberate efforts to grow closer to God (as discussed in previous lessons), and it consists of *ascending* to meet with God on his holy hill. The Songs of Ascents cover many aspects of the upward journey. The psalm we'll look at in this lesson, Psalm 122, addresses the issue of worship. And what it says has as much value for your students today as it did for the Hebrews thousands of years ago.

Stepping Back

The Psalms represent true, heartfelt worship that strips away form, style, and programming to focus on the sole purpose for our adoration—the existence of God.

Church. It's an institution put into place and sanctioned by God. It's his mouthpiece to the world. It's his beloved bride.

So how did the church get such a bad name?

Well, for a start, by not being flexible with changing culture. The church took a bad rap from teens. They weren't allowed to sing their music during worship (rock). They weren't allowed to wear their clothes (jeans). They weren't allowed to speak their language (non-thee and -thou). Lately, however, churches have made a concerted effort to make worship more inviting, more all-encompassing, more culturally relevant,

continued next page

Stepping Back (cont.)

without sacrificing or watering down the truth. As a result many youths are realizing that, far from being boring, worship can be engaging, uplifting, filling, and thrilling.

Besides, God has decreed it. He tells us to worship. He wants us to worship. He commands us to worship.

Why is that? Why isn't it enough for us to go sit in the woods, stare at a tree, and become one with God's creation? Why isn't it enough for us stay at home, listen to a radio preacher, read a good Christian pop-psychology book, and whisper a prayer or two? Why is it so important to ascend God's hill and worship him side by side with other Christians?

First, worshiping God saves us from the evils of idolatry. Everyone worships something. Worshiping God fills the inevitable void and causes us to focus on the only person or thing truly worthy of our worship—God himself.

Second, worship unites us with a larger community, that of the universal Christian church. Especially in today's world, religion gets the label of being a great divider. "Religion" may in fact divide us—but worship unites us.

And third, worship

continued next page

▶▶▶ Opener (large-group option) ▶▶▶▶▶▶▶▶▶▶▶▶▶▶▶

Why worship?

You'll need...
- whiteboard
- markers

When you're ready to begin your meeting, tell kids that you want to make some pro and con lists. Say something like—

> **This week we're going to talk about worship. Some people might think worship and church are the same thing. When we talk about worship in this lesson, we'll be talking about what happens during the Sunday morning church service—the music, the preaching, the drama, the Lord's Supper,** [and whatever other worship elements you have in your church]. **I want you to think about the pros and cons of worship.**

Invite students to call out their ideas. Have someone record them on the whiteboard in two distinct columns. The answers can be actual events in your worship service (the dramas are good) or they can be the results of attending worship (we learn more about God).

When your lists are complete, ask some of these questions—

- **Why do you think God wants us to worship?**
- **What is the best thing about worship for you personally?**
- **Why do you think there are so many different styles of worship?**
- **Do you think one style is better or more correct than another? Explain.**

▶▶▶ Opener (small-group option) ▶▶▶▶▶▶▶▶▶▶▶▶▶▶▶

Worship à la carte

You'll need...
- paper
- pencils

Divide students into groups of four. Tell them that they are in charge of a Sunday morning worship service. It's their job to determine what should be included and to be able to explain why the things they chose are important to worship. They can include ideas that are not usually done at your church.

When students are finished, have them share their ideas with the group. Then ask the following questions—

- **What kinds of things do you think God wants us to include in worship? Explain.**
- **What shouldn't be in a worship service? Why not?**
- **What do you think the ultimate purpose of worship is?**
- **Do you think God is ever be unhappy with our worship? Explain.**

Then say something like—

Worship is a central issue to our lives as believers. In worship, we have the opportunity to stand in God's presence to tell him how we feel, ask him how he feels, and glorify him with singing, giving, and learning from his Word. Today I'd like us to learn more about why and how we worship God.

Stepping Back *(cont.)*

lifts our minds about ourselves. The world, for adults and students alike, is driven by the desire to get more, to move faster, and to pack more and more into smaller amounts of time. Worship helps us stop and take the time to look outside ourselves.

These are things your teens to know. These are things that Psalm 122 has something to say about.

▶▶▶In the Book ▶▶▶▶▶▶▶▶▶▶▶▶▶▶▶▶▶▶▶▶▶▶▶▶▶▶▶▶

God and only God

Begin the lesson with words like these—

Everybody worships something. Some people worship their jobs. Some worship their possessions. Some worship personal image. Some worship God. Why is God supposed to be the only object of worship for a Christian? We're going to look at some Psalms that talk about that.

Group your students into fours. Hand out copies of **God and Only God** (page 112) and pencils. Give students time to look up the verses and finish the sentence for each one. If time is limited, you can assign each group a set of verses to look up. Then call them together to review their responses. Ask questions like these—

- **What did you learn about God from these verses?**
- **Why do you think God wants us to actively worship him?**
- **If we don't take the time to worship God, what do you think we would worship instead?**

You'll need...
- copies of **God and Only God** (page 112)
- pencils
- Bibles

▶▶▶What it all means (personal-inventory option) ▶▶▶▶▶▶

Worship is...

Like many other aspects of the Christian life, worship can be done both in a large group and privately. We pray together. We pray privately. We read the Bible together. We read the Bible privately. We worship together. We worship privately. But how? What things can you do by yourself to worship God? I want you to take a few minutes to think about private worship.

You'll need...
- copies of **I Worship...** (page 113) (cut into two sections)
- pencils

Hand out copies of **I Worship**... (page 113) and pencils. Give students a few minutes to work on the questions. Then ask the following questions—

- **Is there a difference between personal worship and corporate worship? Explain.**

- **Is personal worship more important than corporate worship? Or is corporate worship more important that personal worship? Explain your thinking.**
- **Can you think of times when Jesus worshiped corporately? Privately?**
- **What are the benefits of corporate worship over private worship? Of private worship over corporate worship?**

▶▶▶What it all means (small-group option)▶▶▶▶▶▶▶▶▶▶

You'll need...
- copies of **Holy Connections** (page 114)
- Bibles

Holy connections

Have students gather into groups of four. Hand out copies of **Holy Connections** (page 114), then allow the kids plenty of time to discuss the questions on the sheet. Close this session by having groups sharing their responses. Sum it up with words like these—

> **Did you notice that this psalmist wasn't concerned with where he worshiped or what he wore? He was only concerned about connecting with God. That's the bottom line when it comes to worship.**

▶▶▶What it all means (leader-talk option)▶▶▶▶▶▶▶▶▶▶

Nada

That's right. There's nothing here. Skip ahead to the closing to see why...

▶▶▶Closing▶▶▶▶▶▶▶▶▶▶▶▶▶▶▶▶▶▶▶▶▶▶▶▶▶▶

Stop the talking already, and worship!

Rather than talking about worship, do it. Worship. We all know that experience is the best teacher. Use students to help lead the worship service where appropriate.

Let the worship reflect your church's tradition *and* stretch them some. Here are basic elements you may want to use, in whatever order you choose—

- Read the Bible. You could use several different passages, including a praise psalm, words of Jesus, and thoughts from the epistles.
- Music. If you have a youth worship team, invite them to prepare some songs to lead and perhaps a special presentation. Otherwise you can lead. Be sure to use songs that focus on God, his attributes

(majesty, faithfulness, love, graciousness) and our desire to know him better.

- Prayer. Ask a student to prepare for this ahead of time. Give him specific ideas to pray about and suggest he write out what he wants to say.
- Communion. Be sure to follow your church's guidelines for this sacrament. If possible, have students serve the communion elements.
- Testimony. Have one or two students share briefly about what God is doing in their lives. Be sure they are prepared ahead of time. Have them practice in front of you at least once.

For additional worship ideas, you can get help from *Creative Meetings, Bible Lessons, and Worship Ideas for Youth Groups* and *Worship Services for Youth Groups* (Jim Marian), both published by Youth Specialties.

Add other worshipful activities of your choosing. *Be sure to plan the service ahead of time.*

Close the service with a prayer, perhaps like this—

> **God, you're awesome. You are wondrous. You are mighty, loving, and good. We can't even begin to tell you how much we adore you. You're everything to us. We want to know you better and worship you more fully. We want to learn how to love you more each day. Thank you for loving us, for saving us, and for giving us a reason to live. Amen.**

God and Only God

Read the following verses and complete the sentence.

Verses	We worship God and only God because he—
Psalm 8:3, 4	
Psalm 46:1	
Psalm 47:7, 8	
Psalm 57:10	
Psalm 62:1, 2	
Psalm 93:3–4	
Psalm 96:4–6	
Psalm 103:1–5	
Psalm 144:2	
Psalm 145:8, 9	

I Worship

Worship isn't just a group activity. Worship is a private affair, too. Think about yourself and God, and then fill in the blanks below—

I can worship God when–

I can worship God by–

I will worship God because–

I Worship

Worship isn't just a group activity. Worship is a private affair, too. Think about yourself and God, and then fill in the blanks below—

I can worship God when–

I can worship God by–

I will worship God because–

Holy Connections Psalm 122

Before you read these psalms, discuss—

- Why is worship important?
- When have you felt like you were connecting with God in a worship service?
- When have you felt like you were *trying* to connect with God, but couldn't?

Read Psalm 122.

Verse 1

- Why would David rejoice when others invited him to go to the temple?

Verses 2-5

- Describe the different people you worship with—the "tribes" mentioned by the psalmist—people you don't normally spend time with but who are part of the same family in worship.
- How does worship unite us?
- Why does it sometimes divide us instead?

Verses 6-9

- How does worship provide peace and security?
- What else does worship offer us?
- How can you get the most out of every worship experience?

Resources from Youth Specialties

Youth Ministry Programming

Camps, Retreats, Missions, & Service Ideas (Ideas Library)
Compassionate Kids: Practical Ways to Involve Your Students in Mission and Service
Creative Bible Lessons from the Old Testament
Creative Bible Lessons in 1 & 2 Corinthians
Creative Bible Lessons in John: Encounters with Jesus
Creative Bible Lessons in Romans: Faith on Fire!
Creative Bible Lessons on the Life of Christ
Creative Bible Lessons in Psalms
Creative Junior High Programs from A to Z, Vol. 1 (A-M)
Creative Junior High Programs from A to Z, Vol. 2 (N-Z)
Creative Meetings, Bible Lessons, & Worship Ideas (Ideas Library)
Crowd Breakers & Mixers (Ideas Library)
Downloading the Bible Leader's Guide
Drama, Skits, & Sketches (Ideas Library)
Drama, Skits, & Sketches 2 (Ideas Library)
Dramatic Pauses
Everyday Object Lessons
Games (Ideas Library)
Games 2 (Ideas Library)
Great Fundraising Ideas for Youth Groups
More Great Fundraising Ideas for Youth Groups
Great Retreats for Youth Groups
Holiday Ideas (Ideas Library)
Hot Illustrations for Youth Talks
More Hot Illustrations for Youth Talks
Still More Hot Illustrations for Youth Talks
Ideas Library on CD-ROM
Incredible Questionnaires for Youth Ministry
Junior High Game Nights
More Junior High Game Nights
Kickstarters: 101 Ingenious Intros to Just about Any Bible Lesson
Live the Life! Student Evangelism Training Kit
Memory Makers
The Next Level Leader's Guide
Play It! Over 150 Great Games for Youth Groups
Roaring Lambs
Special Events (Ideas Library)
Spontaneous Melodramas
Student Leadership Training Manual
Student Underground: An Event Curriculum on the Persecuted Church
Super Sketches for Youth Ministry
Talking the Walk
Teaching the Bible Creatively
Videos That Teach
What Would Jesus Do? Youth Leader's Kit
Wild Truth Bible Lessons
Wild Truth Bible Lessons 2
Wild Truth Bible Lessons—Pictures of God
Worship Services for Youth Groups

Professional Resources

Administration, Publicity, & Fundraising (Ideas Library)
Equipped to Serve: Volunteer Youth Worker Training Course
Help! I'm a Junior High Youth Worker!
Help! I'm a Small-Group Leader!
Help! I'm a Sunday School Teacher!
Help! I'm a Volunteer Youth Worker!
How to Expand Your Youth Ministry
How to Speak to Youth...and Keep Them Awake at the Same Time
Junior High Ministry (Updated & Expanded)
The Ministry of Nurture: A Youth Worker's Guide to Discipling Teenagers
Purpose-Driven Youth Ministry
Purpose-Driven Youth Ministry Training Kit
So *That's* Why I Keep Doing This! 52 Devotional Stories for Youth Workers
A Youth Ministry Crash Course
The Youth Worker's Handbook to Family Ministry

Discussion Starters

Discussion & Lesson Starters (Ideas Library)
Discussion & Lesson Starters 2 (Ideas Library)
EdgeTV
Get 'Em Talking
Keep 'Em Talking!
High School TalkSheets
More High School TalkSheets
High School TalkSheets: Psalms and Proverbs
Junior High TalkSheets
More Junior High TalkSheets
Junior High TalkSheets: Psalms and Proverbs
Real Kids: Short Cuts
Real Kids: The Real Deal—on Friendship, Loneliness, Racism, & Suicide
Real Kids: The Real Deal—on Sexual Choices, Family Matters, & Loss
Real Kids: The Real Deal—on Stressing Out, Addictive Behavior, Great Comebacks, & Violence
Real Kids: Word on the Street
Unfinished Sentences: 450 Tantalizing Statement-Starters to Get Teenagers Talking & Thinking
What If...? 450 Thought-Provoking Questions to Get Teenagers Talking, Laughing, and Thinking
Would You Rather...? 465 Provocative Questions to Get Teenagers Talking
Have You Ever...? 450 Intriguing Questions Guaranteed to Get Teenagers Talking

Art Source Clip Art

Stark Raving Clip Art (print)
Youth Group Activities (print)
Symbols, Phrases, and Oddities (print)
Clip Art Library Version 2.0 (CD-ROM)

Digital Resources

Clip Art Library Version 2.0 (CD-ROM)
Ideas Library on CD-ROM

Videos & Video Curricula

EdgeTV
Equipped to Serve: Volunteer Youth Worker Training Course
The Heart of Youth Ministry: A Morning with Mike Yaconelli
Live the Life! Student Evangelism Training Kit
Purpose-Driven Youth Ministry Training Kit
Real Kids: Short Cuts
Real Kids: The Real Deal—on Friendship, Loneliness, Racism, & Suicide
Real Kids: The Real Deal—on Sexual Choices, Family Matters, & Loss
Real Kids: The Real Deal—on Stressing Out, Addictive Behavior, Great Comebacks, & Violence
Real Kids: Word on the Street
Student Underground: An Event Curriculum on the Persecuted Church
Understanding Your Teenager Video Curriculum

Student Resources

Downloading the Bible: A Rough Guide to the New Testament
Downloading the Bible: A Rough Guide to the Old Testament
Grow For It Journal
Grow For It Journal through the Scriptures
Spiritual Challenge Journal: The Next Level
Teen Devotional Bible
What Would Jesus Do? Spiritual Challenge Journal
Wild Truth Journal for Junior Highers
Wild Truth Journal—Pictures of God